A Session by Session Guide to Life Story Work

Life story work is a term often used to describe an approach that helps looked after and adopted children to talk and learn about their life experiences with the help of a trusted adult. This book is an essential step-by-step guide for carers and professionals seeking to carry out life story work with a traumatised or vulnerable child in their care.

Underpinned by positive psychology and drawing on up-to-date research and real-life practice, the book offers a sound theoretical understanding of life story work as well as a practical and easy-to-use programme of sessions. Each session covers the equipment and information needed, a consideration of who is best placed to carry out the work, and answers to commonly raised questions. Also discussed are age-appropriate approaches and ideas for extending each session into other activities and methods to make it more feasible for life story work to be a shared activity between two or three adults who know the child well.

This book gives professionals and carers the confidence to carry out life story work in a way that is sensitive to the child's needs and positive for their self-perception and relationships.

Dr Gillian Shotton is an Educational Psychologist in Northumberland with a specialist remit for working in the children's homes as well as carrying out work in schools. Gillian is also a field tutor on the doctorate course in Educational Psychology at Newcastle University and has written a number of books and journal articles.

"A useful and practical book that describes a gentle approach (which is both simple and sophisticated) which is likely to in-fill emotional holes in the life history of a young person who is likely to have been maltreated."

Dr R. J. (Sean) Cameron, writer and psychologist.

A Session by Session Guide to Life Story Work

A Practical Resource to Use with Looked After or Adopted Children

Gillian Shotton

Routledge
Taylor & Francis Group
LONDON AND NEW YORK

First published 2021
by Routledge
2 Park Square, Milton Park, Abingdon, Oxon OX14 4RN

and by Routledge
52 Vanderbilt Avenue, New York, NY 10017

Routledge is an imprint of the Taylor & Francis Group, an informa business

© 2021 Gillian Shotton

The right of Gillian Shotton to be identified as author of this work has been asserted by her in accordance with sections 77 and 78 of the Copyright, Designs and Patents Act 1988.

All rights reserved. The purchase of this copyright material confers the right on the purchasing institution to photocopy pages which bear the photocopy icon and copyright line at the bottom of the page. No other parts of this book may be reprinted or reproduced or utilised in any form or by any electronic, mechanical, or other means, now known or hereafter invented, including photocopying and recording, or in any information storage or retrieval system, without permission in writing from the publishers.

Trademark notice: Product or corporate names may be trademarks or registered trademarks, and are used only for identification and explanation without intent to infringe.

British Library Cataloguing-in-Publication Data
A catalogue record for this book is available from the British Library

Library of Congress Cataloging-in-Publication Data
Names: Shotton, Gillian, author.
Title: A session by session guide to life story work : a practical resource to use with looked after or adopted children / Gillian Shotton.
Description: Abingdon, Oxon ; New York, NY : Routledge, 2021. | Includes bibliographical references.
Identifiers: LCCN 2020018525 (print) | LCCN 2020018526 (ebook) | ISBN 9780367557874 (hardback) | ISBN 9780367235222 (paperback) | ISBN 9780429280160 (ebook)
Subjects: LCSH: Adopted children–Psychology–Handbooks, manuals, etc. | Narrative therapy–Handbooks, manuals, etc. | Autobiography–Therapeutic use–Handbooks, manuals, etc. | Psychic trauma in children–Treatment–Handbooks, manuals, etc. | Children–Institutional care. | Social work with children.
Classification: LCC HV875.3 .S47 2021 (print) | LCC HV875.3 (ebook) | DDC 362.734–dc23
LC record available at https://lccn.loc.gov/2020018525
LC ebook record available at https://lccn.loc.gov/2020018526

ISBN: 978-0-367-55787-4 (hbk)
ISBN: 978-0-367-23522-2 (pbk)
ISBN: 978-0-429-28016-0 (ebk)

Typeset in Century
by Swales & Willis, Exeter, Devon, UK

An interactive, collaborative approach helpful for those:

- who have experienced trauma, neglect and abuse
- who are in the care system
- who have experienced domestic violence
- who are refugees

Contents

Preface	ix
Introduction	1
A narrative approach to life story work	17
Research around the effectiveness of using a narrative approach	21
How to use this book	27
Session 1: Establishing the ground rules and feelings cards	39
Session 2: The Tree of Life (Part A)	47
Session 3: The Tree of Life (Part B)	59
Session 4: A map of all the places you have lived	67
Session 5: Birth certificate	73
Sessions 6 and 7: Co-constructing the story so far	79
Session 8: Stones in a jar: acknowledging different types of memory	91
Session 9: Origami hearts	97
Session 10: The Team of Life, part 1: values	109
Session 11: The Team of Life, part 2: identifying their team and goals	117

Session 12: The Team of Life, part 3: tackling problems 135

Session 13: Therapeutic stories 145

References 157

Appendix 1: Tree outline 165

Appendix 2: Strength cards 167

Appendix 3: Feelings cards 177

Appendix 4: Jar of stones activity 181

Appendix 5: Team of Life, football pitch outline 183

Preface

The inspiration for this book

In my work as a psychologist, working with young people in care, I have found that many of them have had little, if any, life story work carried out with them. Many of them have had multiple placements and often have scant recollection about when they occurred and with whom. They often have developed misconceptions about why placements changed or why they first came into care. They frequently blame themselves for what has happened to them, for the abuse or neglect they have experienced, for being placed in care to start with and for placements ending, which then influences how they see themselves. These thoughts and ideas contribute to dominant stories that develop about being worthless, unlovable and unacceptable.

The perception of there being little life story work being carried out with young people in care is borne out in the research literature (e.g. Gallagher & Green, 2012; Willis & Holland, 2009). This suggests that there is a lack of consistency in life story work being carried out for young people in care, unless they are going to be adopted, when life story work becomes a statutory obligation.

Why should this be the case? There seems to be a variety of reasons, which include a lack of time for social workers to carry out the work, as well as carers and other professionals lacking the confidence to undertake such work. There is a strong fear about getting it wrong and causing harm rather than healing and helping.

Life story work is a term used to describe an approach that helps people to talk and learn about their life experiences with the help of a facilitator. It allows them to develop a more coherent narrative about their life. For young people in care, it can help them to understand more about the reasons for them coming into care or for changes of placement. It can also help them to become more aware of their own emotions towards the people who have been significant for them in their lives.

Life story work has been used with individuals and groups in a range of settings. To name but a few examples, it has been used: with young people in care (Fahlberg, 2006; Rose & Philpot, 2005; Ryan & Walker, 2016; Willis & Holland, 2009); with people who have learning disabilities (Hewitt, 1998, 2000; Kristoffersen, 2004); with older people on medical wards and in nursing homes (Clarke, Hanson & Ross, 2003; Hansebo & Kihlgren, 2000); with adults who were brought up in an institution (Cozza, 2006); with refugees (Hughes, 2014; Jacobs, 2018); with young Muslim women (Elhassan & Yassine, 2017); with young people who have experienced trauma (Vermeire, 2017); and with young people living with cancer (Portnoy et al., 2016).

I have been significantly influenced by narrative psychology, which emphasises a person's individuality, their strengths and resilience, rather than solely looking at the difficulties they present with. In helping young people to make sense of their past, I was very aware of the danger of retraumatising them by simply inviting them to tell and retell a single-story account of their difficult life experiences. White (2005) explains that, by doing this, we invite a problem-saturated story that is internalised. A thin description of what has happened emerges, which then can come to define them in unhelpful ways. Using a narrative approach, the past is acknowledged, but there is an emphasis on how the young person has responded to those difficulties and the skills they have developed as a result, so that they do not just see themselves as the passive victims of trauma but recognise the strengths and resilience they have shown in the face of hardship. As my reading, research and practice have developed in this area, I have realised more how this narrative-based approach to life story work has utility and validity not just for young people in care, but for other vulnerable groups too, such as refugees and victims of domestic violence, family breakdown and conflict.

This book provides a guide for others wanting to undertake life story work using a narrative approach by giving a session-by-session guide. The aim is to give people the confidence to carry out this work with a young person without feeling overwhelmed or daunted, but also to be able to do it in a safe and meaningful way. It also makes it more feasible for life story work to be a shared activity between two or sometimes even three facilitators who know the young person well.

I would like to see this approach being used to help individuals in a variety of settings, to help them appreciate themselves and others around them, develop a greater understanding of their past and look to their hopes for the future.

Introduction

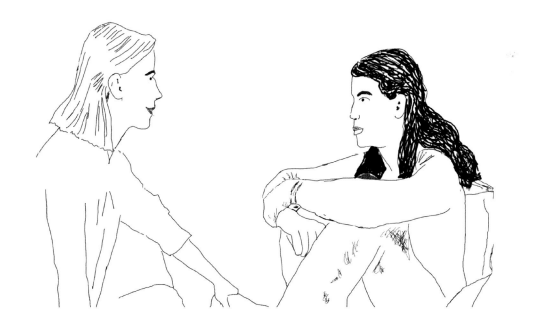

Defining life story work

Life story work is a term often used to describe an approach that helps young people to talk and learn about their life experiences with the help of a trusted adult. It often involves recording relevant aspects of their experience in the form of a book, film, audio record or computer file. According to Ryan and Walker (2007), it is not necessary for life story work to result in an end product; the process itself is the most important factor in yielding benefits for the young person. However, a product is of some benefit in that it becomes a useful record to refer to later. Life story work should be ongoing as the young person grows and develops (Rose & Philpot, 2005). As the child changes and grows, their understanding of what happened in their life will also change. The life story work that might have been carried out with them as a young child should be revisited and explored again, as their interpretation of events may have altered, and they may require different types of information about their past. There will also be new chapters to add as they continue to live, and changes take place. Life story work should not be viewed as being static, something that has happened and now is at an end; rather, it should be viewed as being ongoing, as a dynamic and helpful process throughout life.

Variations in life story work

Life story work has been reported in a range of social care and health settings: with young people (Aust, 1981; Beste & Richardson, 1981; Cook-Cottone & Beck, 2007; Fahlberg, 2006; Rose & Philpot, 2005; Ryan & Walker, 1985, 2007; Willis & Holland, 2009); with people who have learning disabilities (Hewitt, 1998, 2000; Kristoffersen, 2004); with older people on medical wards and in nursing homes (Clarke, Hanson, & Ross, 2003; Hansebo & Kihlgren, 2000); and with adults who have grown up in institutions (Cozza, 2006).

Evidence suggests that there is little consistency, even within particular geographical areas, as to whether life story work is carried out and how the work is undertaken. There are wide variations in terms of what constitutes life story work (Atwool, 2017; Baynes, 2008; Harper, 1996; Willis & Holland, 2009).

Life story work with young people in care

Life story work with young people in care has been carried out by a variety of professionals, including social workers, family placement workers, therapists, clinical psychologists and carers. Different approaches and types of involvement are described throughout the literature. There are variations in the level of participation that the young person experiences. For some young people, a life story book is created for them and presented to them, with the young person having little involvement in its creation. For others, there may be little in terms of an end product, but a pile of messy drawings may represent a meaningful and important piece of work with a young person (Baynes, 2008). The literature also describes methods that are more in depth and therapeutic, often carried out by psychologists or specialist social workers specifically trained in using such approaches (Harper, 1996; Henry, 2005; Rose & Philpot, 2005); others suggest less therapeutic, more factual approaches that carers have undertaken after some training (Beste & Richardson, 1981).

A case study

In one article by an adoption social worker (Nicholls, 2003, p. 32), the story of Sandra (now 40) is told, which highlights the importance of keeping tangible memories safe.

> Sandra was placed in the care system at two months old. She then spent the next eighteen months between the care of her birth mother and several different foster carers. After that she spent the next seven years moving from placement to placement. She then resided in a children's home for a year before being adopted at nine years old. The adopters were given copies of relevant court documents which gave some details about Sandra's past and were also given a postcard which listed her placements. The earliest photo Sandra has of herself is a school photo taken when she was five years old. It is not even an individual photo, but one taken with her class. She has no knowledge of her birth family or tangible memories of what she was like as a baby to nine years old. She doesn't know when she learnt to walk, talk or ride a bike. All she knows is her mother's name and date of birth.

This case study highlights the importance of safeguarding tangible memories for young people in care. The conclusion that Sandra may have come to, because nobody recorded and kept significant memories for her, is that she is of little worth; that she wasn't loved or cherished enough, perhaps that she wasn't good enough to be worth someone safeguarding memories of her young personhood, thus adding to the feelings of rejection she already has to deal with from her experiences (Rohner, 2004). These are devastating conclusions to come to in terms of one's self-perception and self-worth. Conclusions that, in all likelihood, will have a negative impact on her internal working model: the beliefs and expectations that she develops about herself, others and the world around her (Baumeister, 2005; Bowlby, 1988).

Research and experience suggest that there continue to be many young people in care for whom few tangible memories from various placements are kept and for whom little, if any, life story work has been undertaken (Gallagher & Green, 2012; Willis & Holland, 2009). The Adoption and Children's Act 2002 highlights the importance of the views of young people and requires that, on placement for adoption, they must be given comprehensive information about themselves. The National Minimum Standards for adoption services (Department for Education, 2011) specify that, in preparing a young person for adoption, his/her social worker should be gathering their views in relation to their life experiences to date, which should include constructing a life story book. Although this is in place for young people being prepared for adoption, there is no statutory requirement for life story work to be carried out with young people who are in care.

Some practitioners argue for a more coherent, consistent model of life story work to be carried out, and that it should be a fundamental entitlement for children in care. (Atwool, 2017; Cook-Cottone & Beck, 2007; Nicholls, 2003). A model for life story work that strives to create greater consistency is described by Nicholls (2003). From my perspective, I think that each young person who comes into care deserves to have life story work carried out with them, but this needs to be undertaken in a way that is sensitive to their needs and going to be helpful to them.

A colleague once expressed some distaste for life story work and said that the young people should just be allowed to forget the past. She viewed it as 'digging up old wounds that was unnecessary'. Although I can appreciate this point of view, the problem is that the misconceptions that the young people develop, in the absence of information to the contrary, is often detrimental to their own self-perception and contributes to a negative view that they hold of themselves. There is also research evidence to suggest that life story work is helpful and beneficial to young people (e.g. Gallagher & Green, 2012; Willis & Holland, 2009). Although there is not a great amount of research, and this is acknowledged by various writers (e.g. Connor, Sclare, Dunbar, & Elliffe, 1985; Cook-Cottone & Beck, 2007; Davis, 1997; Mennen & O'Keefe, 2005; Rushton, 2004), what there is points to life story work often being positive and helpful to the young person.

What follows is a review of some of the evaluative research that has been conducted into life story work with young people in care. Many journal articles look at how life story work has been carried out, describing different practices (Aust, 1981; Beste & Richardson, 1981; Connor et al., 1985; Harper, 1996; Henry, 2005; Nicholls, 2003). Other articles are more theoretical, describing the theory underpinning life story work and telling one's own personal story (Cook-Cottone & Beck, 2007; Fitzhardinge, 2008; Treacher & Katz, 2001). There are relatively few articles where a research process is explicitly outlined to explore/evaluate life story work with young people in care (Backhaus, 1984; Gallagher & Green, 2012; Happer, McCreadie, & Aldgate, 2006; Shotton, 2010, 2013; Willis & Holland, 2009); however, only four of these articles explore life story work as the primary intervention (Backhaus, 1984; Shotton, 2010, 2013; Willis & Holland, 2009).

The picture that emerges is that there have been few studies focusing on life story work carried out with young people in care. Some research has explored the views of teenagers and adults on their experiences of life story work (Gallagher & Green, 2012; Willis & Holland, 2009). My research (Shotton, 2010, 2013) gives insight into the carers' and young people's perspective on contributing to life story work through collaborative reminiscence.

Backhaus (1984) recognised back in the 1980s that there had been no formal research into life story work, which then prompted her study. She constructed what she terms 'a questionnaire', but it actually sounds more like a semi-structured interview schedule with open-ended questions. She used this to explore social workers' views on the purposes, benefits, practicalities and limitations of life story books. She then interviewed 15 social workers, 13 women and 2 men, who were known to carry out life story work with fostered children in the USA.

The questions were designed to elicit information on some of the major issues for the young person, including feelings of responsibility for placement, anger about separation, perceptions of parents and low self-esteem. The findings from the interviews were grouped into themes: the uses of life story workbooks, preparing the book, format of the book, problems, effects, issues and success stories.

Each worker had at least three reasons for engaging in life story work using life story books:

- Life story books were frequently cited as being a way of helping young people to understand and deal with what had happened to them, to help them retrieve the parts of their lives they had lost through their numerous moves, and give them the ability to integrate past, present and future.

- The books were perceived as giving answers as well as helping to avoid misconceptions, thus helping the young person to be less likely to engage in fantasies about their past or blame themselves for their move into the care system.

- They were seen as helping the young person feel more in control of their past and so were felt to help them feel more in control of their future.

- Life books were seen as being a preventative health measure, giving continuity and helping the young person develop an intact sense of identity.

- They also felt that the work helped the young person integrate good and bad feelings towards others and themselves.

- The workers thought that the life books also helped the young person to begin to see themselves as being different to their birth parents, whereas prior to the life story work they saw it as inevitable that they would repeat their parents' histories.

- Several workers commented that the books were therapeutic in that they revived memories, decreased anxiety and helped the worker to identify unfinished business on the part of the young person.

- They were viewed as a useful way to get to know the young person and so choose appropriate families for them.

- Many of the social workers reported how proud the young people became of their life story book, wanting to show it to others. Several felt that this was an indication of improved self-esteem. Some workers reported how the young person would often want to re-read the books themselves and use them for comfort.

The article is short and, therefore, does not give a lot of detail as to the views of the social workers or insight into the way they phrased their responses and the language that they used. It refers often to 'several' workers as holding a particular view without giving an idea of how many workers this constitutes. It is, therefore, difficult to make a judgement as to the prevalence of particular views.

Another point to bear in mind is that the sample was confined to social workers who used life story books and who were, therefore, more likely to hold positive views about life story work. It would have been interesting to discover the views of a more random sample of social workers. An important omission is that the young person's views were not represented.

The researcher concludes that life books have been shown to be an excellent concrete tool for discussing the past and helping the young person to work on the feelings connected with life events. Yet these are solely the views of the social workers. It would have been interesting and useful to have heard the young person's and carers' views on the life story work they had experienced, triangulating their perceptions with those of the social workers.

In a study by Gallagher and Green (2012), interviews were carried out with 16 young adults (10 female and 6 male) of 16 years and over, asking about the care they had received in The Orchards (therapeutic children's homes in the UK). A key part of the input in these homes was a focus on life story work. The life story workers used what they termed a 'deep and rich' approach to life story work (Rose & Philpot, 2005), seeing it as a therapeutic tool in addition to the weekly 1-hour therapy sessions each young person received. There were three to five young people in each home, with two or three staff on duty at any one time. It is unclear whether the life story work was carried out by the staff in the homes or by others.

A semi-structured interview schedule was used with the young adults to explore their views. Most of the young people in the sample had received at least 36 sessions of life story work over a period of 18 months. The majority of them had been placed in the homes at a relatively young age (mean = 8.4 years), and most had left when they were 11–13 years of age. The average duration of each interview was 135 minutes. One of the main topics covered by the interview questions was life story work.

All the young people stated that they valued the life story work that had been carried out with them, and some reported that it had been especially helpful. Quotes from the young people are offered, giving useful insight into their particular views.

An indication of the young people's positive attitudes towards life story work was evidenced by how well some of them had looked after their life story books over a long period of time, how familiar they were with them and still referred to them, their decision to carry on with life story work in their next placement and their intention to carry out life story work with their own children.

It is reported that the interviewees said that life story work had helped them in three main ways:

1. In acquiring a more accurate picture of their lives before they entered the home
2. In facilitating relationships with the staff in the home and with carers in subsequent placements
3. In dealing with the emotional and behavioural challenges they had faced.

Another benefit was that life story work could trigger positive memories for the young people, as their life story books often contained memories of happy times. Life story work was challenging emotionally for some of the young people interviewed, because of the complexity of their lives and because sometimes they did not want to recall upsetting experiences. One young person reported sticking a piece of paper over one part of her life story book that she did not want to be reminded of.

Some were pleased with the way their life story book had been organised and the effort that had gone into it. For others, there was some dissatisfaction over the life story work they had received. They felt that they had not been sufficiently involved in it, that it had been done for them rather than with them, or that it lacked depth.

It is not made clear in the research how many of the young people expressed each of these views, so it is difficult to get an idea of the prevalence of views expressed. The researchers link their findings to those of Willis and Holland (2009), who found a similar commitment to life story work among the young people in care they interviewed.

Gallagher and Green acknowledge that their work may not have highlighted other problems that young people in care can have with life story work. In Willis and Holland's (2009) study, for example, some young people in care expressed how they sometimes found life story work tedious. However, Gallagher and Green's overall conclusion is that young people value life story work and can benefit from it.

Willis and Holland (2009) carried out semi-structured interviews with 12 young people aged 11–18 (five female, seven male) on their experiences of life story work in one local authority in South

Wales. The young people reflected on the emotional aspects of the work and the new information they had gained about their own histories. In contrast to the study by Gallagher and Green (2012), here the young people had all experienced very different styles of life story work, and the degree of input varied enormously. Interview findings were organised into three interconnecting themes:

1. The form and purpose of the life story work carried out
2. The emotions associated with the work
3. The constituents of life story work – that is, the physical objects that made up the record.

The content and level of input varied greatly. Most of the young people had memory boxes as well as some sort of written record. Amber (15) had done all the work herself, focusing on writing an account of the abuse she had experienced before coming into care. Three young people had used the pre-printed BAAF book (Camis, 2001) 'My Life and Me'; others had a more personal record in a scrap book or photo album and seemed to have spent more time in discussion with a practitioner. Some were taken on trips to get photos, whereas others did not leave their home as part of the process.

A number of the young people's views are quoted, which helps to develop a greater insight into the views expressed. For example, Harry (15), felt that life story work was about 'yourself, your personality and family … [going] into greater detail about our histories and stuff like that'. His interests, such as cars, sports and animals, were incorporated into his life story book; the researchers outline that this helped to reflect his character.

All the young people expressed positive feelings towards life story work, but some found the process tedious at times and perceived it as being a chore. There are reports from two young people who found it boring and felt it was a bit like homework that they did not want to do. Many reported positive feelings about learning new information about their past through the life story work, although it is not specified how many young people expressed this view.

Betty (17) had no photos or mementos from two of her foster placements, which highlights how young people's experience of foster care and the memories stored remain varied. Several young people saw life story work as being an ongoing project and envisaged a future purpose for it. Harry planned to show it to his children when he got older. Ellie also suggested she would show some, but not all, of her life story book to her children. Several reported that they had shown it to people who had visited their homes and were interested. Amber had ripped her account up as she did not want anyone to read it. However, she said that, if she had kept it, she would now have shown it to those closest to her.

Several of the young people gave some insights into the emotions they experienced when engaging in life story work. For example, David (11) had a photo of himself buried in sand at the beach and was reminded of his love for the sea and his pride in burying himself. He appeared to relive the emotions as he was reminded of this special time. Amber had written part of her life story to explore her negative experiences and said that it had helped her as it had 'taken her mind off crying and stuff'. Sid (11) felt that it was not helpful to have sad memories recorded as, 'you read your life story book and you then feel sad again so what's the point?'.

As well as the verbatim quotes from the young people, I also appreciated the inclusion of pseudonyms for each of the participants, which helped to identify each speaker and their unique voice. This meant I could look at the range of views from each participant to build up more of a picture of them as an individual.

The strength of this is that it gives insight into the variety of experiences that young people have of life story work; the weakness is that, as a result of this variation, it does not help us to evaluate any particular approach to life story work, which would have been helpful for informing future practice and training.

Although, inevitably, there are some mixed feelings among the young people in the studies, what emerges is that life story work has generally been perceived by social workers and young people as being positive and delivers benefits on a number of different levels.

Streams of psychology that inform our thinking on life story work

There are a variety of streams of psychology that inform our thinking on how life story work might be working from a psychological perspective to help people. Aust (1981) writes about life story work as being the beginning of a re-education of the young person's beliefs in a manner congruent with Ellis's rational emotive therapy (Ellis & Grieger, 1977). She describes how a young person's reaction to separation and loss produces painful feelings of anger, abandonment, shame and rejection. These feelings affect how young people see themselves and distort their interpretation of events. They often come to see themselves as being inherently bad and unlovable. Life story work is thought to help in identifying, challenging and re-educating these beliefs.

The trauma of rejection and separation impacting on the young person's sense of worth is also outlined by Harper (1996). She puts forward the view that life story work can help young people to accept their past and, therefore, they can then feel in control of it, rather than it controlling them. In this way, they can move on, putting the past behind them. This links in with ideas around developing a sense of agency or self-efficacy (Bandura, 1977). Harper uses a non-directive play therapy approach to life story work, rooted in psychotherapy.

The work of Bowlby (1980, 1988) on separation and attachment is acknowledged by Henry (2005) as providing a foundation for understanding how young people experience and respond to loss. Bowlby (1988) outlined how it was through the young person's relationship with a significant carer that their internal working model developed. An internal working model contains all one's expectations and beliefs about the world, about oneself and about other people. The contrast between the beliefs and expectations of a young person with a secure attachment and a young person with an insecure attachment is shown in Table 0.1.

Table 0.1 Contrast between internal working models (Bowlby, 1988)

Beliefs and expectations of a young person with a secure attachment	Beliefs and expectations of a young person with an insecure attachment
I am good, wanted, worthwhile, competent and lovable	I am bad, unwanted, worthless, helpless and unlovable
Caregivers are responsive to my needs, sensitive, caring and trustworthy	Caregivers are unresponsive to my needs, insensitive, hurtful and untrustworthy
The world is safe, and life is worth living	The world is dangerous, and life is not worth living

The underlying thinking is that the young person needs to reconcile the traumas and separations in their life to make a successful transition to a permanent placement. The young person must also be allowed to grieve the losses they have experienced (Bowlby, 1980, 1988), and much of the difficult, acting out and aggressive behaviour often seen in young people in care is understood as being due to unresolved loss. Life story work is seen as being a useful tool for helping young people to reconcile the traumas they have experienced and grieve their losses, which will then help them to be able to move on.

The model of life story work put forward by Cooke-Cotton and Beck (Ryan & Walker, 2007) is rooted in narrative psychology. They draw on theory outlined by Nelson and Fivush (2004), who describe how the family and cultural stories that young people hear help them construct their own autobiographical narrative and thus contribute to their sense of identity, helping them to make sense of their past, present and anticipated future (McLean, 2005; Nelson & Fivush, 2004). Parents reminiscing, telling their young person stories about times in their earlier lives, provide young people with information about who they are and how others feel about them, and this then helps to develop their sense of self.

For younger children, autobiographical remembering relies on the parent/carer prompting and sustaining the focus of the conversation (Habermas & Bluck, 2000). The years between complete dependence on the carer and the individual being able to independently construct their own memories are described by Nelson and Fivush (2004) as the years of co-constructed memories. Parents help the young person to construct a coherent life narrative, so that they develop a clear understanding about where they came from, how others felt about them, their place in the family and in the world. There is evidence to suggest that reminiscences and the co-construction of life memories may be related to secure attachment, the development of a sense of self in the past, and how past self relates to current self (Fivush, Haden, & Reese, 2006; Fivush & Vasudeva, 2002; Kulkofsky & Koh, 2009). The life story is thought of as being sculpted continuously, becoming the organising structure that carries the self (Cook-Cottone & Beck, 2007).

Young people in care do not live with people who can verify their past and so miss out on the opportunity to create a positive and coherent life narrative (Beste & Richardson, 1981). Life story work is seen as helping to fill the gap; the work allows for the co-construction of a coherent life narrative that will then help the young person develop a stronger sense of identity.

It is useful and interesting to look at the differing perspectives regarding the psychology underlying life story work. My own interpretation is that none of the perspectives seem to be in conflict, but rather each offers a slightly different emphasis or way of understanding how life story work might function. In line with Ellis's rational emotional therapy, life story work has the potential to impact on young persons' beliefs about themselves. From a psychotherapy perspective, life story work also has the capacity to help young people accept and understand their past and feel more in control of it, developing their sense of agency and so allowing them to move on.

> This is what happened to me, this is my story. I am responsible for some parts of my story and others are responsible for other parts.

Drawing on Bowlby's work, life story work has the facility to help the young person reconcile the traumas and separations they have experienced and allow them to grieve their losses. From a narrative perspective, life story work has the potential to help young people develop a coherent life narrative, so contributing to their sense of self. It also has the potential for other stories, which acknowledge the young person's strengths and resilience, to be strengthened or 'thickened'. I see the different streams of psychology as giving different insight into the ways that life story work may be working psychologically, rather like a stained-glass window. Each coloured pane of glass has value in itself and gives a slightly different perspective, but each is also helpful in understanding and appreciating the whole picture.

Stained glass windows at the Sagrada Familia in Barcelona

A narrative approach to life story work

The approach this books focuses on is informed by narrative principles. A narrative approach seeks to be respectful and non-blaming and centres people as the experts in their lives. It views problems and adversity as being separate from the person and highlights the skills, competencies, values and abilities that people have that can help them to reduce the influence of problems in their lives. Fundamental to using a narrative approach is maintaining an attitude of curiosity towards the person you are working with and being willing to ask questions to which you don't know the answers.

A central idea within narrative psychology is that we are continually engaged in interpreting and making sense of our experiences. The stories we have about our lives are created by linking events together in a meaningful way and making sense of them. The narrative is the thread that weaves the events together to form a coherent story (Morgan, 2000). We all have many stories that exist simultaneously about different aspects of our lives, such as stories about ourselves, our abilities, our relationships, our interests, our failures.

For example, a person could have a story about their being a good cook. They string together many events that have happened around cooking and interpret these as being a demonstration of their skills in this area. They might remember cooking as a child with a carer and doing well in helping out; they might think about how they learned to make something difficult, such as making choux pastry and how that turned out well and was appreciated by those who ate the creation. They might remember how they are able to make a smooth bechamel sauce with ease, whereas others find this difficult. To form this story of themselves as being a good cook they select certain events that fit with this particular plot, giving them priority over other events that do not fit quite so well, such as the time the cake sunk or the bolognaise sauce was a tasteless disaster. Important in all of this are others' reactions, as we do not make stories in isolation from those around us. The things that others say and do impact on our interpretation of events and, therefore, the stories that we create. The smiles and appreciation shown by others for the cake that was baked play a significant role in the formation of a story about being a good cook.

As more and more events occur and are selected, they are put together into a dominant story. The story becomes more comprehensive and 'thickens'. Events that fit a dominant story tend to be given more attention and are more likely to be remembered; events that do not fit a dominant story may be disregarded or forgotten.

A dominant story not only affects us in the present, but also has implications for our future actions as it affects how we interpret events. An individual may have a story about being a failure at trying new things, and subsequent events will be interpreted in the light of this dominant story. Narrative therapy seeks to help people explore the stories they have and strengthen, or 'thicken', alternative stories that are more helpful to them (Freeman, Epston, & Lobovits, 1997; Morgan, 2000).

The approach outlined in this book utilises this narrative approach to help young people explore and begin to tell stories about themselves. Stories that not only acknowledge the difficult events they have experienced, but also highlight positive relationships in their lives, stories about their strengths and the resilience they have shown in the face of adversity.

In the absence of a consistent carer, young people in care often grow up without a coherent narrative. They develop their own, often flawed, interpretations of why they came into care and often have an overriding sense of guilt as many assume that they must have been to blame in some way. That they did something, or did not do something, that made events unfold as they did, or that they could have done something that would have prevented things happening as they did. Because of these dominant stories that they hold, many young people carry an underlying sense that there must be something wrong with them. That they are unlovable, unacceptable and inherently bad.

When a narrative approach to life story work is used, the young person's story is acknowledged, explored and clarified, but there is also an emphasis on exploring together the overlooked, forgotten stories around the young person's strengths and the resilience they have shown under difficult, often horrendous, circumstances. When young people are helped to make sense of their past, there is the danger of their being retraumatised simply by being invited to tell and retell a single-story account of their difficult life experiences. White (2005) explains that, by doing this, we invite a problem-saturated story that is internalised. A thin description of what has happened emerges that then can come to define them in unhelpful ways. Treacher and Katz (2001) write about how life story books can sometimes silence the difficulties experienced by adoptees by not allowing them enough space for exploring troublesome feelings and fantasies. They outline how, often, the life story that is constructed adheres to a prevailing narrative that has the following basic elements:

- Your birth parents loved you but, because of their personal circumstances, they were not able to look after you
- Your adoptive parents chose you because they love and value you
- You have had terrible life experiences, and our job is to help you overcome those experiences.

The writers outline how often such narratives prevail in order to help the professional make sense of the pain the young person has been through. They point out that the story is unlikely to mention how administrative mistakes, a lack of available carers or practice failures have led to difficulties for the young person. A certain narrative is expected to emerge that is essentially positive and reparative, but that may not be the most helpful or tell certain aspects of the story.

Using a narrative approach, the past is acknowledged, but there is an emphasis on how the young person has responded to those difficulties and the skills they have developed, so that they do not just see themselves as the passive victims of trauma but recognise the strengths and resilience they have shown in the face of hardship. The story is not constructed by others for them, but they are active participants in the process.

Research around the effectiveness of using a narrative approach

There is evidence to suggest that using a narrative approach is an effective and helpful intervention for children and young people who are vulnerable owing to the experiences they have had. The Tree of Life narrative methodology, which is utilised in this book, has been carried out with a variety of different groups. An article by Elhassan and Yassine (2017) describes how it has been used with young Muslim women living in Australia. They found that the approach opened up a space for alternative stories and helped to build a stronger sense of community. The Tree of Life methodology has also been used to help refugees. Jacobs (2018b) describes how it was used to help unaccompanied refugees on a Greek island speak about their difficulties in ways that were not retraumatising but instead made them feel stronger. An article by Hughes (2014b) describes the use of the Tree of Life with refugee families, with children and adults having sessions together. She describes how the approach allowed them to develop empowering stories about their lives that were rooted in their cultural and social histories. From this secure base, they were then able to develop shared congruent solutions to their problems.

The Beads of Life narrative-based approach has been used to support young people with cancer. It helps them tell preferred stories of their identity to create a safe place to stand from which to talk about their cancer journey. In positioning the young people as experts in their lives, it aims to change the relationship the young people have with cancer, reducing its negative impact by lessening isolation. Using the approach also helps the medical staff get to know the young person apart from the cancer; there is evidence that this creates hope for the future and improves the quality of care (Portnoy, Girling & Fredman, 2016).

Using a narrative approach has also been found to be effective when working with children who have experienced traumatic life events such as abuse, neglect or witnessing domestic violence (Vermeire, 2017). Often in such situations, the child exhibits behaviour problems, and the adults decide that what the child needs is to be able to talk about the trauma they have experienced. Children themselves are often unconvinced about the helpfulness of talking; they often experience that talking leads to more trouble, and that adults are not always reliable. Many children who experience trauma lose touch with a valued sense of who they are and reach negative conclusions about their identities and their lives. Their sense of self becomes so diminished that it becomes very difficult for them to give any account of what they value in life (White, 2006, in Vermeire's article, 2017). Vermeire has found that using a narrative approach in which the therapist–child relationship is suspended for a while by use of role play allows for new conversations to become possible. The unspoken can be said from another role or position, and new stories can be brought in from that vantage point. From a different position, the child can discover that they have ideas, knowledge and responses to certain experiences. They can reconnect with their values.

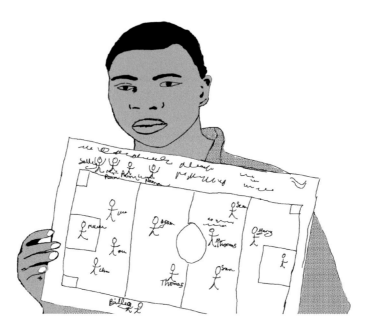

In his book *Collective Narrative Practice*, Denborough (2008) describes how using the 'Team of Life' narrative-based approach helped Sudanese refugees make sense of their experiences using the medium of football. The methodology helps individuals focus on the relationships that they have now, as well as those that have been important to them in the past. It also helps them to talk about their achievements and the resilience they have shown, as well as their hopes for the future. A key element of using a narrative approach is generating documentation that serves as a vehicle for talk, reflection and sharing. In this way, the sessions do not just end when the time ends; there is an ongoing reminder of the talk that occurred that can be utilised in a number of ways, making the impact of the work more powerful and enduring. Denborough describes, across two books, *Collective Narrative Practice* (2008) and *Do You Want to Hear a Story?* (2018), how narrative practice has been used to help a diverse range of groups of people, including:

- Syrian refugees
- Children and young people who have experienced abuse
- People experiencing anxiety and depression
- Those who have experienced bullying
- Children and young people in school to enhance self-esteem and challenge racism
- Villagers affected by an earthquake in Kashmir
- Women who have experienced grief
- People who have experienced sexual abuse
- Adults living with HIV
- People with learning disabilities
- Older adults

- Children and young people with type 1 diabetes
- Hard to reach parents.

I hope you have found it interesting and reassuring to read about the research that evidences the validity of using a narrative approach with vulnerable young people. For me, it is important to know that there is evidence that using a particular approach is helpful and beneficial. I do not want to be stabbing in the dark with what I think might be a good idea. I want to know, and I want you to know as well, that the methodology has evidence behind it, particularly when we are thinking of vulnerable young people.

How to use this book

In the first three sessions, the Tree of Life methodology is used. This means that a large focus in these sessions is on the young person's strengths and their hopes and dreams for the future. This creates a sense of safety and helps to establish positive relationships, where the young person knows that the professional working with them understands more about them, what they are good at and what they would like in the future. Having established this context and from this place of security, the focus can move on to explore the young person's past and the stories they have about their past. Although the focus moves on to the past, in each session there are questions that allow you to open up conversations with the young person about their strengths and the resilience that they have shown, while acknowledging potential ongoing uncomfortable feelings and difficulties.

A team approach

The approach in this book is designed so that undertaking the life story work ideally does not fall on to just one person, but rather there is a small team of the young person, one of the main carers and one or two other professionals, such as the young person's social worker or a psychologist. Some sessions will be more emotionally demanding than others and so there needs to be communication between the team as to who might be better placed to do which session. In this way, carers can do some of the sessions, but allow the social worker/psychologist/other relevant professional to undertake some of the more emotionally demanding sessions, such as the story of how a child who is fostered came into care, or sessions that explore the abuse or violence that the young person experienced. Often, it is helpful for both the carer and the other professional to be present in the session with the young person. This is helpful for a number of reasons:

- The carer can comfort the young person with an arm around them if the young person needs it.
- It sends a strong message that everyone knows the young person's story and values their strengths and resilience.
- It means that the carer can be prepared for more sensitive nurturing over the next week, if a session has been particularly difficult and emotional for the young person, as they will have experienced the content first-hand.

The guidelines for each session discuss how emotionally demanding it might be and offer helpful approaches to adopt to difficult questions that may arise. Frequently, not everyone will know all the answers to the young person's questions, and it is OK for the adults to admit this and to feel comfortable saying, 'I don't know the answer to that, but we can ask … or we can try and find out by …'. Or, it might be that you have to admit that you will not be able to find out the information.

The use of metaphors, as described by Davies and Hodges (2017), can offer the young person a way of thinking about difficult and sensitive experiences and feelings. Metaphors give the young person a way of understanding their experience by helping them to organise what they experienced. The same metaphor may provide useful ways of thinking about a variety of experiences. Closely involving the carer means that the metaphors can become part of an ongoing, shared understanding and dialogue that will reduce shame and help the young person to feel accepted. For example, the metaphor of a tree weathering storms and continuing to stand is a useful one, as all of us experience storms in our life, big and small. As the life story work goes on, the young person, carer and professional will experience continuing interpretation of the narrative and reinterpretation.

There is evidence that using a narrative approach helps to improve current relationships and helps young people understand more about why they feel and behave in certain ways now. An important emphasis, stemming from positive psychology, is on strengths and the adaptive qualities the young person has demonstrated. These adaptive qualities have helped them to survive even though they may now be problematic in a different context. The aim is to strengthen and thicken stories around the young person's strengths, the resilience they have shown, as well as their hopes and dreams for the future. The approach this book facilitates, and advocates, is that the life story that emerges from the work should be co-constructed by the young person and the adult(s) involved.

Order of the sessions

The sessions in this book are numbered for ease of reference, but they do not necessarily have to follow a strict order apart from the first three. The idea is that you read through each session and decide in conjunction with the young person and other professionals/carers where it might be most helpful to go next. It is recommended that you start with the first three sessions as suggested in the order here. These sessions are an ideal starting point for the work you are about to embark upon with the young person. They are helpful for getting to know them, but, even if the carers and professionals know the young person well, they act as a useful starting point. They set the tone for the sessions that are to follow and allow you to develop tools and ground rules that will be invaluable in subsequent sessions.

They allow you to develop a working agreement for the sessions with the young person. It is always important to make the way you are going to work explicit, rather than assuming everyone understands the ground rules. For example, you might assume that the young person knows that no question is a silly question, for example, but clarifying this in the working agreement makes it explicit and helps the young person to feel safe. Tools such as the Tree of Life and the emotions cards, which you complete in these first three sessions, will be useful for referring to in subsequent sessions. It is always useful as well in subsequent sessions to remind the young person of the working agreement you have developed together.

The Tree of Life

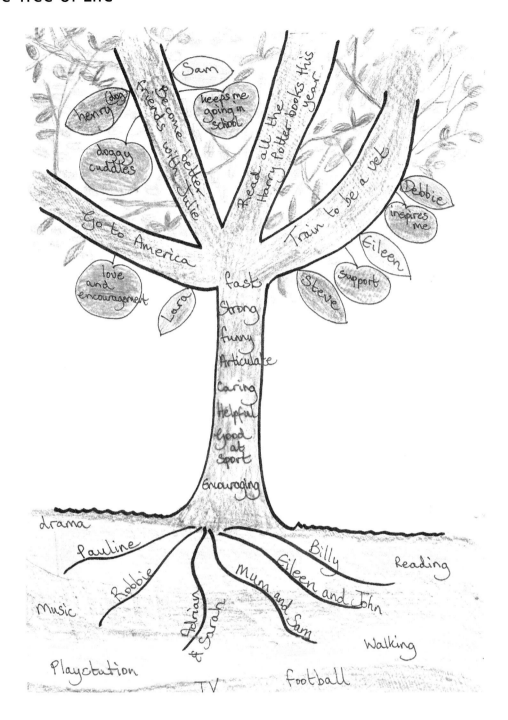

A key tool that we will be using throughout the sessions is the tree of life metaphor, which you begin in Session 1, but is carried on in other sessions and is a useful overall mind map or framework to refer back to, from which the young person can understand and locate all the life story work that is being carried out with them.

Each session comes with a guide that outlines what materials you will need for the sessions and what resources to use. You will need to spend a bit of time preparing yourself before each session, so you have everything you need to hand.

A 20-pocket presentation book is a good medium for displaying the life story work. But, here again, this is just a suggestion. The file or folder that is chosen to put the work in should reflect the taste/interests of the young person involved so that they find it attractive and it reflects their style.

Time scale

Sometimes, the work may get started and then need to be stopped as the young person was not ready for it at that time. Carers and professionals need to dedicate time slots over a period of weeks so that the work has sustained momentum, and relationships, particularly between the young person and the professional(s), are established and strengthened. I would suggest that at least ten sessions are planned in order to carry out this work. You may find that each session takes more than one meeting with the young person to complete. This might be because you are working with a young person who wants to talk a lot, or maybe the young person has a short concentration span so you have to keep the interaction time shorter (e.g. 30 minutes rather than an hour). This is absolutely fine. The value of the work is not in completing and ticking off that you have completed all the sessions, but rather the talk and subsequent understanding that is developed through the work.

Before you start

Before starting the life story work, you need to find out about the young person and their history. You may have found out some information already from relatives, the young person themself or from other sources. Wherever possible, it is a good idea to check out the information you have with other documentation. This is where social work files or other documents are very useful. For example, Uncle Robert may remember that the young person went to live in foster care for 6 months when it was actually a couple of years. People's memories are not always so reliable. Often, this is not deliberate deception but just because people do not remember things accurately. So, as well as talking with relatives, you need to spend some time with the official documents that detail a young person's story, if they exist of course. For some groups, there may be little or no documentation.

Your research might involve going to a social work office or wherever the records are held. Unless you are the young person's social worker, you will probably have to read the documents in a supervised room so that the information remains secure, so go prepared with paper and pens to note things down.

Social work files are often difficult to decipher. Acronyms are used, and things get misfiled. You may come across multiple pieces of information about the same event, or multiple copies. It is not necessarily straightforward by any means. A good plan is to take with you some big pieces of flip chart paper and pens. This is handy particularly if a couple of you are going to read through the files, as then you can start to put your findings together on the flip chart.

The column headings in Table 0.2 are just suggestions but allow you to chart information from the documentation you look through, to build up a coherent picture. This can also be quite revealing – 'Oh so I didn't realise that that was going on in mum's life whilst he was being fostered over in Stanton'. It is a good idea to use different-coloured pens just to make it easier to read later on and break up the text. It is useful to put the years up the side at the start, just to give yourself a time frame to focus on, but leave plenty of space between the years. Often, you find that many events are documented for one year and then there is a gap in terms of the amount of information for other years. I would say as a guide to space out the years over two pieces of flip chart paper.

Table 0.2 Key events chart

Year	Location	Key events	Health	Education
2020	Tinal House, Alenden	Sam doing well making positive relationships with residential carers	Sam trialled with ADHD medication	Sam doing well at local school, some behaviour incidents but interventions in place
2019				
2018		Sam placed in residential care at Tinal House children's home in Alenden		
2017		Foster placement breaks down; the reasons for this seem unclear	CAMHS confirm ADHD diagnosis	
2016	Sandy Lane, Widrunton	Sam placed with Sandra and Jim foster carers in Widrunton. Holly placed in another area as no places available locally	ADHD assessment	Reports of difficult behaviour in school Sam unsettled, often violent towards others
2015	Palmers Grove, Ashton	Mum involved with multiple partners. Evidence of substance abuse and neglect		
2014		Sam and Holly back with mum. Still involved with Jim. This relationships then finishes		
2013	Holly Street, Derben with Sue Halpe		Sam assessed by CAMHS for ADHD – inconclusive	School reports of Sam doing well with reading but sad and very possessive of others
2012				
2011		Sam and Holly taken into care. Go to live with foster carer Sue Halpe in Derben		
2010	Palmers Grove, Ashton	Accounts of neglect. Sam seen in street, asking neighbours for food		
2009		Mum with various partners, some known sex offenders. Accounts of domestic violence witnessed by Sam		Sam showing disturbed behaviour in school. Often disruptive
2008	Cader Lane, Sidwell			
2007		Sister Holly born		
2006				
2005		Sam born 8lbs, Jefferton Hospital		

Obtaining the young person's consent

Before starting, you need to talk with the young person about what the life story work will entail and ask them if they are happy to do this work and explore their past, present and hopes for the future. You can explain to them that the sessions will be fun, interesting and sometimes creative, which may appeal to them. If they like to work on the computer, you can use this as a format for the work to take place. If, having understood what it might involve, they say that they do not want to, or do not feel ready to, engage with this work, we need to respect that and come back to them at a later date to make the same offer. It is important for the young person to feel that they have agency and that this is something they have chosen to do, rather than it being forced upon them.

Session 1: Establishing the ground rules and feelings cards

You will need:

- A range of pictures depicting different facial expressions. These can be cut out of old magazines, newspapers, and so on, or downloaded from the internet. The type and style of image – cartoon, photo and so on – will depend on the age and interests of the young person. Important emotions to include: happiness, relief, feeling peaceful, joy, anger, sadness, jealousy, anxiety, resentment, nervousness, panic. See Appendix 3 for feelings cards that you could use here if you don't want to make your own with the young person

- Paper/card

- Coloured pens/pencils

- Pritt stick

- Scissors

- Life story workbook. This could be photo album style or a display book with transparent pockets. The young person can then do a picture for the front cover and useful documents – photos, certificates, maps, mementos and so on – can be stuck on to A4 paper to go inside each pocket.

Emotional demand: low to medium

Although you can never be completely certain, as you do not know what is going to come up or be particularly sensitive to a young person in terms of emotional sensitivity/emotional demand, this session should be towards the lower end of the scale.

This first session is designed to get you going in a safe way so that you and the young person know what the ground rules are for your sessions together and everyone feels safe and comfortable with them.

Establish a working agreement (ground rules) for the sessions

Explain that, in order for us all to feel safe, we need to have a working agreement. You may find that 'working agreement' is better than the phrase 'ground rules' as it does not sound quite so akin to school, with the mention of 'rules'. Here are a few suggestions:

1. Breaks are OK

    It should be made clear that, if at any time during the session they need to have some time out or it's all too much for them, it's OK to have a break. Sometimes the young person may not return from the break, but this should be respected, and it should be accepted that they needed that time and can start again afresh on another day.

2. All questions are permitted

    Another important ground rule is that there are no stupid questions. We need to make it clear that it is fine to ask questions, but we may not have all the answers. If we don't have all the answers, we will try to find out. Both you and the young person need to be aware that sometimes the information may not be available, and this can be frustrating.

3. Keep to time

    Both you and the young person need to start at the agreed time. The young person needs to know that the sessions will last no more than 1 hour. An ideal time frame is 50 minutes, and then you can use the final 10 minutes of the hour to make a few notes or use it for discussion with the carer/other professional involved.

4. Confidentiality

    You can let them know that things that are said in the sessions will be confidential; however, if there is anything that is said that indicates they are in danger, or have been in danger in the past, that information will need to be passed on. You'll be checking with them what they're comfortable with being written/shown in their life story workbook and who will be able to read it.

    Ask them for any suggestions they have for the working agreement or any questions they have. It's a good idea to chart the working agreement in felt pens so that you can bring it along to subsequent sessions as a reminder.

Working agreement

- We'll both try to get here on time.
- There's no such thing as a silly question.
- It's fine to have a break.
- What's said here stays here, unless it's something that indicates that you or anyone else may be in danger, either now or in the past.
- I'll check out with you what is ok to share and how to word your book.

Make a feelings chart

Many young people do not talk about how they are feeling on a regular basis. It is not something they are used to. They may have a limited emotional vocabulary; other than happy and sad, they may not be familiar with expressing other emotions or understand what they feel like. During the life story work sessions, it is likely that the young person will experience a number of emotions, some good, many uncomfortable. Some common emotions that might be experienced during life story work are sadness, anger, worry/fear, nervousness, confusion, rejection, resentment, jealousy, happiness, relief, a sense of calm, joy, peace.

It should be made clear to the young person that it is OK for them to express how they are feeling in the sessions and that it is permissible. To help them to do this, you can collaboratively make a feelings chart that displays a range of emotions, and they can then have this to hand in the life story work sessions. The young person can then simply point to the emotion when they experience it. Depending on the confidence of the young person in drawing and their propensity to get involved in art and craft activities (some love it, some don't), you can roll out this activity in different ways.

Bring along images of a range of emotions from the internet, magazines or other picture resources. If they like drawing, the young person can have a go at drawing their own version of these emotions. Get them to draw them on a chart or on small cards. If they do not wish to draw, they can simply stick the images on to a chart or download them from the internet directly. In this way they can search for celebrities or cartoons that they are particularly keen on.

Ending each session

It's important to end each session by agreeing the next time and date for the next session and giving the young person a little bit of positive feedback for anything they did well in the session. Descriptive and specific praise is most effective in this context. Where possible, try to start your sentence with 'I notice', rather than the more valuative 'I like' – for example, 'I notice that you chose blue for the sad picture, that really gives a sense of someone who is feeling sad', rather than the more general, 'Great drawing!'

Session 2: The Tree of Life (Part A)

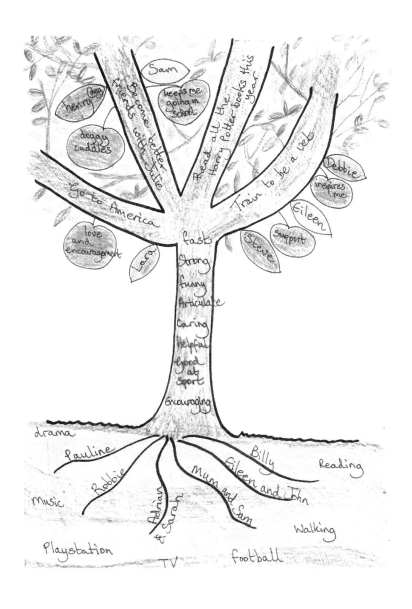

You will need:

- Images of different trees. You can download images of famous trees from the internet, or use photos, magazines, and so on
- Paper (A4 or A3, or lining paper, if you want to give them the freedom to draw a much bigger tree)
- A photocopy of the outline of the Tree of Life (see Appendix 1)
- Strength cards (see Appendix 2)
- Coloured pens and pencils.

Emotional demand: low to medium

Although you can never be completely certain, as you don't know what is going to come up or be particularly sensitive for a young person, in terms of emotional sensitivity/emotional demand, this session should be towards the lower end of the scale.

The Tree of Life

Throughout the sessions, you are going to use the Tree of Life as a tool for bringing together many different aspects of the young person's life story, their past, present and future. The Tree of Life has been used within a narrative approach as a tool for facilitating conversations that strengthen, or thicken, stories about positive aspects of a person's life, as well as acknowledging and clarifying the past. The tree also serves as a metaphor that will be useful to refer to in subsequent sessions. The young person can see where the other sessions fit in terms of their Tree of Life. It's a great starting point for life story work as it acts as a map showing where you are up to. The methodology balances a focus on the past with stories of the present and hopes and dreams for the future. This balance between past, present and future tends not to be found in other accounts of life story work that I have researched. The tendency is to view life story work as just being the story of what happened to you in your past.

Another advantage of the Tree of Life is that, if you don't know the young person very well, it gives a good insight into their character and their ideas for the future. It helps you to get to know them and them to get to know you without yet venturing too much into their past and the stories it contains.

> The different parts of the tree represent different aspects of an individual's life:
> - Trunk: the strengths you see in yourself; others can add to this too
> - Branches: hopes and dreams for the future
> - Leaves: people who are important to you now
> - Fruit: the gifts that people give you, perhaps of encouragement or love rather than material gifts
> - Roots: the people who have influenced you in your past
> - Ground: the activities that you enjoy doing.

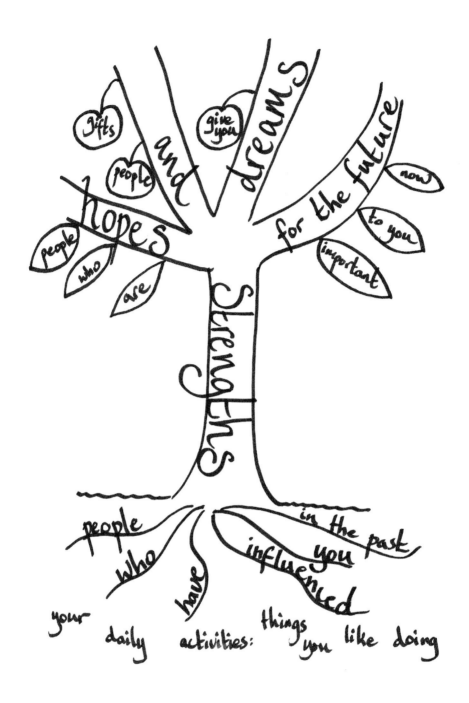

All trees experience storms at some point or other, and this analogy allows you to explore together the storms, the difficult times, a young person has experienced, emphasising the strengths and resilience they have shown during those times.

The Tree of Life can be completed over a number of sessions, and the drawing of the various parts of the tree allows conversations to develop that build stronger, 'thicker stories' about a young person's unique qualities, hopes for the future, their life now and the people who are important to them, as well as looking into their past and the people who have influenced them.

Introduction

Use photos or images of different trees from all over the world. Or go on a walk to look at various trees. If the temperature outside is warm, you might like to do this activity sitting under a tree. Share photos of different trees and encourage discussion. Which is their favourite, which is yours, and why?

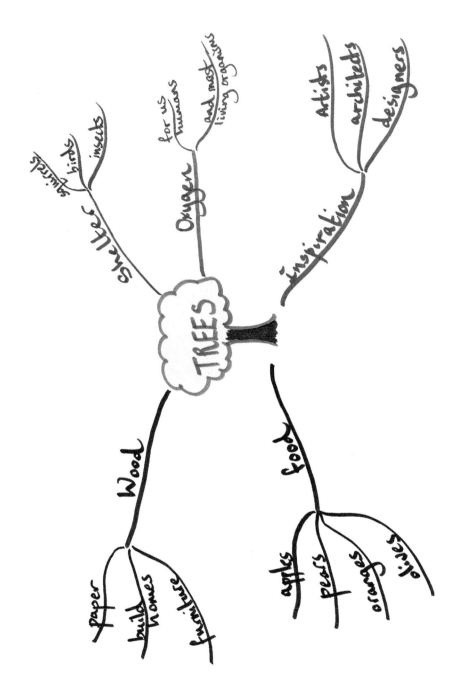

Create a mind map with the young person about trees.

Discuss with the young person

'Have you ever looked at a tree and admired how beautiful it is, the shelter it provides to animals, the colours that change throughout the year?' You then might like to go on to discuss trees that have been significant for the young person, maybe a tree they used to like to climb or look at.

Explain that they are going to be drawing a tree that will chart different aspects of their life. This can be a joint activity, with both you and the young person drawing your trees simultaneously. This helps to normalise the activity and can support the young person to appreciate that we all have different strengths, hopes and dreams, and that everyone's are valuable. Alternatively, you can just focus on helping the young person with their tree.

For some young people who are nervous about drawing, they might prefer to have an outline of the tree drawn for them. Often I find that the young person draws the tree outline without leaving sufficient room for the words that it needs to contain. To give them an idea of an outline that works, either show them, or photocopy for them, the outline in Appendix 1. You can enlarge this to A3-size paper or leave it as A4. For many young people, the opportunity to draw and get creative is welcomed. Make sure you take with you some good-quality pens and pencils of different colours and decent paper. It's important that this is seen as a special and valued exercise, for which you need drawing materials that demonstrate that value as well.

Once you have the outline of the tree, the next step is for them to identify their strengths, which will then be written in the trunk of the tree.

The trunk of the tree: identifying strengths

Many young people find it difficult to identify their strengths. If you ask them what they are good at, the likelihood is that you might not get much in response. To help them get started, you can use strength cards such as the ones shown in Appendix 2, which they can first sort into piles to identify 'those that are like me', 'those that are not like me' and 'those that are sometimes like me'.

Questions that are useful to elicit conversations that 'thicken' accounts of the young person's strengths:

'Tell me more about that.'

'When did you notice you were good at …?'

'How did you learn to be good at that, who taught you?'

'Who else knows that you're good at …?'

Once the strengths have been identified, they can be written in the trunk of the young person's tree. It's useful to emphasise that these may change and be added to over time. The analogy of a tree is useful here, as a tree is a living organism that is growing and changing all the time, just as we grow and change. While the young person is writing in their strengths, you can be creating your own tree of life, writing your strengths in the trunk as well. This then allows it to be a more collaborative session. It gives the message that this is not just something they need to do because they need help: it is an appropriate and good exercise for everyone. It also allows you to experience how difficult it can be sometimes to identify your own strengths. In many cultures, and particularly in the UK, people are not brought up to talk about their strengths. There is a very strong message given out that you should never brag about what you are good at, you should always be modest, and so it can feel uncomfortable to talk about yourself in this way and identify positive characteristics or things that you have done well. You can add to the young person's Tree of Life as well, saying, 'Something I've noticed about you is …'.

The branches: hopes and dreams for the future

Once the strengths have been written in, the next step is for the young person to identify their hopes and dreams for the future. This can be the next year or their long-term aims, which may be many years away. The hopes and dreams are written on the branches of the tree. Using the language 'hopes and dreams' is really important as it conveys a sense of optimism as well as a sense of freedom and excitement to select things that might sound practically impossible. If a dream is unrealistic, it doesn't matter – all is allowed, all is permitted. These do not have to be SMART targets (specific, measured, achievable, realistic, timed). It is a chance for the young person to express things that, perhaps, they have never expressed before about the future and what they would like to happen.

This might be as far as you get for this first Tree of Life session, but in it you will have learned much about the young person, and they about you.

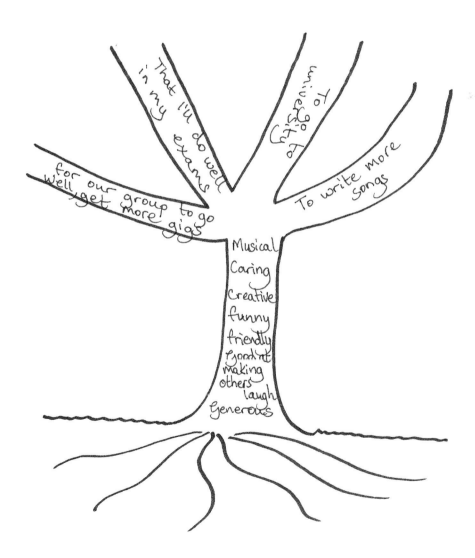

Example of a tree part filled in

In-between sessions: sharing the tree so far with others

There may be others in the young person's life with whom they would like to share their tree so far. This allows them to talk again about their strengths, thickening further those stories, as well as talking about their hopes and dreams for the future. If the young person wants to share their tree in this way, the carer or another person (perhaps a teacher) can also be asked to contribute to the tree by identifying further strengths that the young person may have.

Session 3: The Tree of Life (Part B)

This session completes the other parts of the tree of life.

> You will need:
> - The Tree of Life created so far
> - Pens and coloured pencils
> - The working agreement created in Session 1
> - The emotions pictures created in Session 1.

It's good to have to hand a copy of the working agreement you made together in Session 1, as well as the emotions pictures. Go back over these with the young person, just reminding them of what you've agreed and how they can refer to the pictures, if they like, to express how they are feeling, for regular 'feelings check-ins'.

Leaves and fruit

In the leaves of the tree, the young person identifies people who are important to them now in their lives. In the fruit, they identify the gifts that those people give them. These are usually non-material gifts such as encouragement or love or confidence.

Questions to ask:

- 'Do you have fun with this person?'
- 'What is special about this person to you?'
- 'Would this person like to hear you talk about them in this way?'
- 'Why do you think the person gave you this gift?'
- 'What did they appreciate about you that could have led them to do this?'

Roots and ground

In the roots, the young person identifies people who have influenced them in their past – they can be people who have died or are still alive. This might be family, teachers, friends or others who have had an impact on their life. It can be people who have taught them about themselves or about life. It can also be people who they feel have had a negative impact; they are still part of their roots.

Questions to ask:

- 'Who is the person who you would say has taught you most in your life?'
- 'What things did you learn from them?'

In the ground, the young person identifies the sorts of things that they enjoy doing each day/week. These can be hobbies or clubs, special programmes or people they like watching on screen, games they enjoy and so on.

Questions to ask:

- 'What do you enjoy doing most?'
- 'Do you get a chance to do this activity very often?'
- 'Do you have a favourite song or place at home?'

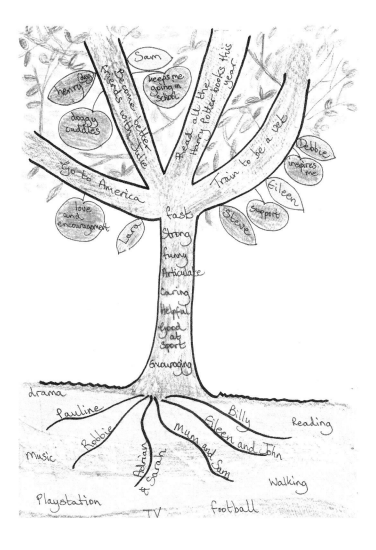

The tree as a framework for further sessions

Explain that in subsequent sessions you are going to be looking together in more detail at the roots of their lives, their past; in other sessions, you will explore the other parts of their tree, the people in their life and what they bring, how they see themselves and their hopes for the future. The tree gives an overall framework so they can see which part you are exploring more about together.

In-between sessions: sharing the tree so far with others

Once again, give the young person the opportunity to share their tree with a significant other in their life. This then allows them to further thicken those stories that they have started to tell with you.

Session 4: A map of all the places you have lived

This session gives the young person an overview of where they have lived geographically. It shows the transitions to different places. In many ways, this can be a good starting point to talking about their life in the past. It is factual, but conversations will inevitably come about through it about why changes of placement and so on occurred.

You will need:

- Details of when and where the young person lived; it may be appropriate to have the addresses

- A map (or maps) that covers all of the geographical locations the young person has lived in. You can use Google Maps to define the area and print out the map. Google Earth and Street View (in Google Maps) are also helpful resources for bringing an address to life

- Pens/pencils.

Emotional demand: low to medium

The map activity in itself is quite factual and tends not to be quite so emotionally charged as other sessions might be. If you and the young person decide to do a road trip around the various locations, this has the potential to be more emotionally demanding for the young person. Actually seeing the places and being near the places where difficult times happened can bring back floods of memories ad uncomfortable emotions. As a team, in conjunction with the young person, you need to decide whether this is something the young person would like and who they would find helpful to be with them on this trip.

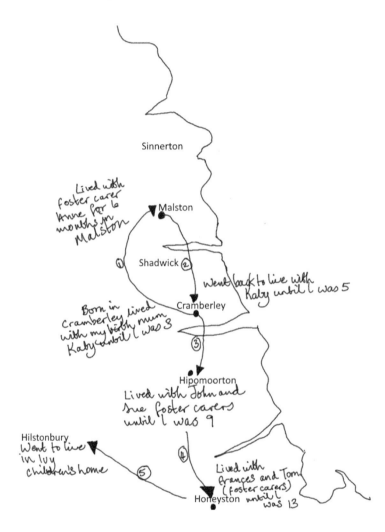

Once you have prepared the map, you can write on it where they lived at various times in their life. The scale of the map depends on where they've lived. You may need to print out a map that shows other countries – for example, when working with refugees – or, if they've only moved up and down the same street, your map might be a street map showing the specific houses. You might need to use a couple of maps. You can either start at the beginning of their lives where they were born and work forwards, or you can start from where they are living now and work backwards.

Questions that might occur:

- 'Why did I have to move from x to x?'
- 'Why could I not have stayed with x?'
- 'What happened in a particular placement?'

Working collaboratively

Depending on the needs of the young person, you could also have a map of the places you have lived in your life to share with them. Once again, this helps to normalise the process of charting your geographical history and also allows them to see that we all have different experiences.

Road trip

Sometimes it can be helpful to physically go to the places and do a road trip round where the young person lived. It is important to bear in mind that some addresses will hold distressing memories for the young person, perhaps some memories that they have not yet disclosed. It may be appropriate and helpful to meet former carers at some of the addresses, but this will require prior arrangement; at others, it may not be helpful or appropriate, and a drive-by or a brief walk along the street is perhaps the best course of action. Care must be taken when planning such a trip. You don't want to put the young person in a dangerous, distressing or awkward situation where they encounter relatives who do not have contact permission. You will need to use your knowledge of the young person, and what happened to them and where, in order to decide on the most helpful approach to take with each location. The young person should also be consulted on what they feel comfortable with. Take along the feelings chart, made in the first session, so that it is easily accessible for the young person to use as a way of expressing how they are feeling as you go. Try to ensure that the trip ends with something nice, such as a trip to a café, ten pin bowling or maybe watching a fun film that evening.

Session 5: Birth certificate

A useful starting point for further sessions where you will chart a family tree with the young person is to spend a session with them looking at their birth certificate. In their book *Life Story Work* (2007), Ryan and Walker describe how, when they first started doing life story work, they thought that the birth certificate would not provoke much attention. In actual fact, it turned out to be of immense interest to the young people and triggered numerous questions. Young people seem to grasp its significance, that it is an official document that shows they were born and that they have an official identity.

> You will need:
> - Working agreement
> - Emotions pictures
> - A colour photocopy of the certificate
> - Glue and paper to stick it into their book.

Emotional demand: medium to high

The emotional demand can be quite high. The young person may or may not be aware of who is identified on their birth certificate as their mother and father. It is a good idea to first check with them if they've been told who is on their birth certificate or if they have seen it before, to avoid any distressing surprises. This is a good session for the professional involved to facilitate jointly with the carer, so that the carer can be there for more emotional support.

Sometimes you may not have access to, or there may not even be, a birth certificate – in the case of refugees, for example. Where the birth certificate is not available, you can still cover information about the start of a young person's life by gathering and using information about their place of birth, birth weight, and so on.

This can be presented to the young person in a form they can relate to – for example: 'When you were born you weighed about 3 kg which is the same as a big bottle [3 litres] of fizzy pop'.

> Questions that might occur:
> - 'Why do we have birth certificates?'
> - 'Why does she/he have a different name to me?'
> - 'Why was I born there, what is that place like?'
> - 'Is that a normal size/weight for a baby?'

Case study: Sam

While looking at his birth certificate, Sam suddenly became very quiet and looked sad. His carer, Sally, asked him what was wrong. Sam shook his head; he couldn't speak. 'Were you expecting to see your dad's name?' she asked.

'I knew his name wasn't going to be on the birth certificate,' Sam replied, 'But seeing no name there on that proper certificate, piece of paper makes me feel …' He pointed to the sad and disappointed pictures on his emotions cards. Sally gave Sam a hug. We both talked about how it was natural and normal to feel sad about aspects of our past. We also talked with him about the likely reasons for the absence of a name. That his father had not been with his mother when he was born, and that his mother's mental health had been very poor at that point, so she may not have had the presence of mind to put the father's name down. Sam continued with the session but was thoughtful. Sally made sure that, later in the day, there were some nice, fun things in store for them. They watched a funny film together and had his favourite dessert. At bedtime, Sam was reassured that, if he wanted to talk about his feelings, that was OK.

Interesting information about birth certificates

It's useful to have to hand some interesting information about birth certificates that you can share with the young person, depending on their age and interest.

Births have been documented across many hundreds of years and in many different countries. The main purpose originally of documenting a birth was for the ruler to know how many people to tax and to know how many men would be available to fight in times of war. The compulsory practice of registering births in the UK goes back to 1875. Before this system of recording births, evidence of births was dependent on the birth being registered by the Church of England.

The birth certificate is signed by the registrar, who is commissioned by the government. The record is stored with a government agency (the General Register Office). If you need a copy of your birth certificate, you can request this. You need your birth certificate in order to apply for a passport.

In the UK, there are two types of birth certificate. A full certificate entitled 'Certified Copy of an Entry' is a copy of the original entry in the birth register. It gives all the recorded details including name, sex, date of birth and place of birth; father's name, place of birth and occupation; and mother's name, place of birth and occupation, as well as her maiden name, if she has one. Certificates issued before 1969 do not show details of the parents' place of birth. Certificates issued before 1984 do not show the mother's occupation. If the father is not named on the birth certificate, this means that he has no legal rights over the child unless the mother allows it through giving her written consent. This could be a salient point for the young person, depending on their relationship with their father and what they want in the future.

The short version of the birth certificate, which is entitled 'Certificate of Birth', shows the young person's full name, sex, date of birth and place of birth. It does not give any details about the parents. It is issued free when the baby is registered. Both versions can be used to verify your identity, but, if you need documentation to verify who your parents are, you will need the full birth certificate rather than the short one.

According to the United Nations Convention on the Rights of the Child (1990), every young person has the right to a name and nationality (Articles 7 and 8). It sets out that every young person should be registered after birth and has the right to a name and the right to acquire a nationality.

Archbishop Desmond Tutu said in 2005 that a person's birth certificate is a small piece of paper, but it actually establishes who they are and gives access to the rights, privileges and obligations of citizenship.

It is estimated that, every year, across the world 51 million babies – almost one in three, are not officially registered. This means that these young people do not have birth certificates and, from a legal point of view, they do not therefore exist. Without a birth certificate, these young people are likely to be poorer and more disadvantaged than their peers. In many countries, if you do not have a birth certificate, you cannot register to attend school, take exams or get vaccinations.

Without a birth certificate, you cannot prove your age, and so you're more at risk of being exploited by being put to work or being treated as an adult in the justice system or being forced to fight in the army of that country. As a girl, you're more likely to be married younger than that country allows or be trafficked.

Case study: Afroza

Afroza is 18 years old and lives in Bangladesh. She is mum to twins who are 11 months old. Because she didn't have a birth certificate, her parents were able to get a fake one and pretend that she was older than she was. This meant she was married at age 15, when the legal age for marriage in Bangladesh is 18.

Sessions 6 and 7: Co-constructing the story so far

The work that you will have carried out with the young person so far will have given you insight into their lives, events that occurred, changes they have experienced, and so on. Now is a good time to start to put that information into a coherent narrative for the young person. This involves you writing the story that encapsulates what you know of the young person's life, from the sessions and the research you have carried out so far, and then using that in these sessions with the young person to check out how the story matches up with their understanding of what happened. In this way, the account that emerges will be co-constructed between the young person and the adults involved. There needs to be a sensitive and honest account of the young person's story about coming into care and the events that led up to this and followed it. Neglect and abuse should be explained in a simple, non-judgemental way. This will probably take at least two sessions' worth of time and may require three sessions.

You will need:

- To have done some preparation work writing out a narrative that encapsulates what you understand of the young person's life
- Emotions cards
- Working agreement.

Emotional demand: high

These are sessions where the emotional impact is often high, and so having a carer present, or other professional who knows the young person well, can be very supportive and helpful. The other adult must have a positive relationship with the young person, as this allows them to hear the telling of the story, the difficult times and the good times, and to reinforce some of the messages you want to give to the young person: that they are acceptable and lovable and that, most probably, they were not to blame for much of what they experienced.

In among the difficulties, it's important to tell any positives that there were.

Case study example: John's story

When you were born your mum was just 16 years old, very young to be having a baby. She didn't know how to look after babies. She had grown up in a very strict family. When she was little there had not been any cuddles or kisses from her mum and dad. They were often very angry with her. When she was 15 she ran away because she didn't get on with her parents and wanted to be free from them. She found some older friends and began drinking alcohol. She met your dad at a party and they were together for two weeks. It was later that your mum found out she was having a baby but she didn't tell your dad. By then she was with another man, Malcolm.

When you were born your mum didn't really know how to look after you in the way that you deserved. She wouldn't have known how to look after any child. She had become depressed and was taking drugs as well as alcohol to try to help herself feel better, except that didn't really work. Malcolm, her boyfriend, was a violent man who used to hit her a lot. Often he hit her in front of you. Of course you were really scared by this and you used to cry and cry.

When you were one your mum had your sister Hannah. Frequently there was no food in the house and you and Hannah didn't have clean, dry clothes to wear. You were both often wet as your nappies had not been changed for some time. It wasn't always that bad but eventually the social workers decided that it wasn't safe or fair for you and Hannah to remain in your mum's care as she couldn't look after you properly or keep you safe and you were put into foster care. Malcolm eventually went to prison for being violent towards another man in a pub.

You and Hannah lived with Sandra and Jack, your foster carers in Holdrum, for three years. From when you were two until you were five. While you were being cared for there, your mum had another baby, Sophie. When you were five the social workers felt that your mum was able to look after you and Hannah again, so you both went back to live with her, where she was living with Clint. Your mum did a parenting course with Clint before you went back, and everyone thought it might turn out ok. Your mum really wanted you back.

> It turned out that your mum was not really able to look after you all very well. Clint was violent towards your mum and was sent to prison for badly hitting and hurting your mum, and you saw your mum being hit.
>
> When you were back living with your mum you used to go to a gymnastics class. Your grandparents used to take you each week and then you'd go to their house for tea.

It's also important to be truthful about the difficult times.

When sharing the story, as you understand it, with the young person, they may have revisions or parts they want to add. In this way, the narrative becomes a co-construction between you and the young person. They may say things that you are not sure are totally true. Unless you have definite evidence to the contrary – that is, that what they have said didn't really happen – then it's important to include these memories as they hold significance for the young person. It's a good idea to frame them as their memories of the time.

John remembers ...

> I remember when I was living with my mum and I was about seven years old, I had to get up and go down to the shop to buy milk and food for breakfast. My mum was still asleep in bed. By the time I got back my little sisters would be up so I would get some breakfast ready for them. Then I would walk Hannah to school and when Sophie was old enough I'd take her to nursery. That meant that by the time I got to school I would be late, and the teacher would shout at me for this. After school sometimes my mum would be there to pick me up and sometimes she wouldn't.

This co-authoring of different times in the young person's life can take a number of sessions. It's important to note as well that it is likely to be emotionally raw for the young person to share about these times. The emotions cards need to be at hand for the young person to use to indicate how they are feeling. It's also a good idea to have an agreed nonverbal signal that the young person can use if they need a break, and to reiterate that breaks are permitted.

Linking back to the Tree of Life, you might like to use the analogy of all trees going through stormy times that often have a lasting impact on them but, with the right sort of support and help, they can stay standing tall and strong. It may be appropriate to outline that they did not deserve to have had the times they have experienced, and that things that happened were not their fault. This can be said to the young person in the session, and then reiterated later and backed up through a therapeutic letter. It's even more powerful if the letter is written from the perspective of both you and the carer who had the opportunity to listen to the story, as you both form an outsider witness team. Outsider witnessing is a practice used in narrative therapy where one or several people are invited to join a session and listen to the story that emerges in the session. Michael White (1995) was the first to develop outsider witnessing practice. Once the story has been heard, the witnesses are invited to comment using a number of outsider witness questions (Christie, McFarlane, Casdagli, & Fredman, 2016). With using a team approach to life story work, you have, in effect, a readymade group of outsider witnesses, usually consisting of the main carer and professional involved.

Outsider witness questions can be used to facilitate a conversation between the professional and the carer that either the young person can sit and listen to or can be written into a letter to the young person.

Questions for the outsider witness team

1. What in particular encouraged or inspired you. What were you drawn to or touched by?
2. What did this suggest to you about the young person's values/hopes/dreams/commitments – what is important to them? What picture or image came to mind from what you heard?
3. Which aspects of your own life resonated with what you heard? Why is this significant to you?
4. Where have you been moved to in your thinking or experience of life or work? How is your life different for what you have heard today? How have you been influenced?

The young person can then be asked to comment on what they have heard from the witnesses. Hearing how their story has influenced others and made a positive contribution to others' lives can be very powerful, opening up space for further positive developments in terms of self-perception.

What follows is an example of a letter to a young person that exemplifies this approach.

Dear John

It was a real privilege to work with you on Tuesday and carry out some life story work with you. Thank you for sharing your memories of that time with us. There were parts of the story that we knew about and other parts that we didn't.

We're sorry John that you weren't looked after properly as a little baby/toddler or when you were a bit older, six to eight years. You had to look after yourself and your younger siblings a lot of the time. You also experienced some very scary times, with people who were not safe for you to be around.

What came to both our minds was your determination to care for those around you John. To look after your sisters even when it was difficult. This really shows how much caring for others is important to you, an important part of your life. Your determination has inspired us both to keep caring for people in our lives who can be quite difficult at times.

Sometimes there are storms in life, and you have experienced periods of your life that have been very stormy. Sometimes a storm is so powerful that it knocks trees over, but you haven't been knocked over John. We were so impressed with how resilient you have been during difficult stormy times and what a fantastic young person you have grown into. You have so many strengths, and hopes and dreams for your future, which is great to see.

Pat and I wanted just to say in writing how immensely proud we are of you.

The type of language that you use and the number of pictures/photos you include will depend very much on the age of the child. A good guide is to look at a typical reading book for their age group and gear your content accordingly. Often, professionals and carers fear going over some of the difficult times the child has experienced, but, if these times are never gone over, misconceptions about what happened and who was to blame are allowed to flourish. The child may also feel more like a monster, as if their story is too hideous for anyone to know about and must be kept secret.

Tracie Faa-Thompson, a dear colleague, wrote and shared a story with 4-year-old Holly who had been through some emotionally distressing times. An abbreviated version of Holly's story follows. Tracie used clip art to illustrate the story in a way that made it appropriate for and understandable to Holly, who was an able child. As with all the case study examples in this book, names have been changed to protect anonymity.

> Holly's 'born to' mummy's name is Emily. When Holly was born Emily was only 16. That's really young to look after a baby so Holly's grandma, Amy (Emily's mummy) helped Emily to look after Holly.
>
>
>
> But Emily and Amy did not get on with one another and they used to fight. Sometimes they even hit one another. Now fighting is a real bad thing to do and when there is a little baby there too, they might get hurt by mistake. Luckily Holly did not get hurt but she easily could have done.

So because there was so much fighting and arguments between Emily and Amy, social workers and health people, who knew Holly very well, were really worried about her. They all tried to help Emily and grandma Amy but they just kept on fighting and arguing and telling tales on one another to the social workers.

Here's another thing, Emily and grandma Amy came from Canada. When you come to live in another country you need permission to stay in the UK for a long time. Emily did not have permission to stay so she had to go back to Canada and grandma Amy stayed in the UK and continued to look after Holly.

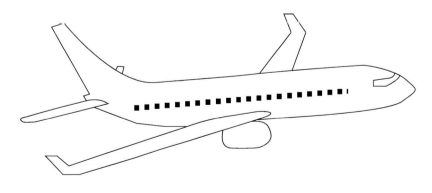

As there were not a lot of places to live grandma Amy had to take Holly to live in a homeless unit. This is where people live while they are waiting for a house to become available.

One night a serious thing happened. The gas taps on the cooker were left on. Not just one but all of them at once. That's really scary because lots of gas can cause a big bang and if that happened the house would have fallen down and the people who lived there might have died or been very badly hurt.

So the police were very worried about Holly and decided it was not safe for her to live there with grandma Amy anymore. So Holly went to live with foster carers.

And guess who they were? That's right, David and Jean. And guess what? David and Jean and their children all loved Holly straight away.

Tracie felt comfortable writing that last part as David and Jean had said to her that they were happy for it go in the story. This is where a team approach becomes really important.

Holly listened while Tracie read through the story and asked questions, especially around the explosion part of the story. Afterwards, David and Jean were not quite sure how much Holly would have taken in, but it soon became apparent that she had a really good understanding of her story and referred back to it again and again, asking questions and making comments about it from time to time. Tracie continued to work with the family and the happy ending to this story is that Holly went on to be adopted by David and Jean.

Session 8: Stones in a jar: acknowledging different types of memory

This activity has been adapted from an idea on the Winston's Wish website. It was suggested to me by a lovely friend and ex-colleague, Caroline Feltham-King. The activity is very practical and provides a way of helping the young person talk about positive memories from their past while acknowledging difficult ones too. This can then help the young person develop a sense of perspective and balance about their past.

> You will need:
> - A variety of different types of stones
> - Smooth pebbles
> - Gem stones
> - Sparkly stones
> - Jagged rough stones
> - A small jar, or jars if you also take part, one for each person.
> - You could go on a trip to collect stones with the young person that could then be used in this session.

Emotional demand: medium to high

Talking about difficult memories can bring up emotions of sadness, shock, anger, betrayal, and so on, that are difficult to deal with. This is balanced, however, by a focus on positive memories as well. The stones themselves offer a useful focus for the session – they can be touched and felt. The rough, sharp stones can be held alongside the smooth and special stones to represent how we all have a variety of memories, of stories in our past, that can be held together. Having the young person's carer there for a hug or comforting touch can be really helpful. It can also be helpful for you and the carer to carry out the activity and share your memories as well, just to normalise that all of us have difficult memories, as well as more positive memories, from our past.

Possible script

So today we're going to think about our past and the stories that we have about our past. Some stories will be happy ones and some will be more difficult or uncomfortable memories. We're going to choose stones to represent these different types of memories.

Present the different stones on saucers for ease of selection. Ask everyone to feel the different stones and look at them carefully. First of all, choose a sparkly stone or a gem stone to represent a happy memory from your past and spend some time talking about that memory with each other. Then choose a spiky, hard, rough stone to represent a difficult or sad memory. Encourage the young person to feel the stone in their hands and describe how it feels. They might observe that it is sharp and rough, and if you press on the sharp bits it can cause pain. Make the connection between that and holding some of these more uncomfortable memories: sometimes they can be difficult to hold, especially if you just focus on them. However, if you put them in the context of lots of other more positive memories, you can have a more balanced perspective. Share with one another about that memory. Finally, choose a smooth stone to represent something ordinary that used to happen in your past, something that perhaps represents everyday life – for example, 'my "born to" mum would always have three spoons of sugar in her tea'.

If discussing times when the young person was not being looked after well by a carer, it may be appropriate to give messages about how their carer could not have looked after *any* child at that time in their life. This is very different from the message that they could not look after '*you*'. The implication is that it wasn't just something about them, the child, that was unlovable or problematic; it is likely that their carer, at that time, would not have been able to look after any child.

You can go on choosing different stones for the jar, but try to encourage a balance between uncomfortable and positive memories. It's a good idea to record what memories were remembered for which stone using the sheet contained at the back of this book (see Appendix 4).

Place the stones in a small jar that can be put somewhere safe. Use your judgement as to whether the young person might be likely to destroy the jar, and, if this is the case, place it somewhere that they do not have independent access to. Alternatively, you could take a photo of the jar as a memento to go in their book.

Session 9: Origami hearts

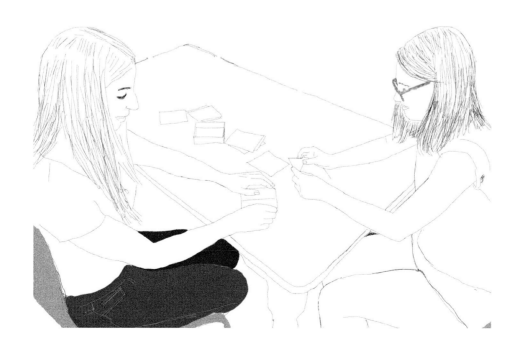

Celebrating people who have had a positive impact

This session celebrates the people in the young person's life who they feel have had a positive influence on their life. They may be people who taught them things, they may be carers, relatives, teachers or other professionals. The key here is allowing the young person time to identify people who have made a difference to their life and reflecting on what they have brought them. The people identified may be still in their life or they may be from the past, people with whom they no longer have any contact.

This session is more appropriate for age 10 upwards, just because of the origami and the tea lights, but use your own professional judgement. You may also decide that the origami element is too difficult or would not interest a particular child. If this is the case, feel free to adapt the activity so that the origami hearts are already made. Similarly, you could remove the tea light element of it if you feel it is too dangerous with a particular child or young person, or you could use battery-powered tea lights.

> You will need:
> - A sheet of paper and coloured pens (on which to brainstorm the names of the people with the young person)
> - Instructions for making origami hearts
> - Squares of origami paper (white one side, coloured the other)
> - Tea lights and tea light holders (about ten; you can use battery-powered tea lights if you are concerned about safety)
> - Candle lighter.

Emotional demand: medium

This session focuses on people in the young person's life who have had a positive impact, and so it may well engender feelings of appreciation and happiness rather than more uncomfortable emotions. Having said that, it's helpful to acknowledge that there are no guarantees with emotions!

Introduction

'In this session we're going to be thinking and celebrating the people in your life who you feel have made a difference, who have taught or brought something into your life and have had a positive influence.'

Refer back to their tree and who they have identified in their roots, as well as on the leaves.

As for all the sessions, make sure you have the feelings chart displayed for the young person and reiterate the ground rules.

On a sheet of paper, either you or the young person can jot down the names of people that the young person identifies. If the young person is struggling to think of people, you can refer back to those they identified on the roots or the leaves of the Tree of Life. They may need some prompting, and so knowledge about their life story is essential here.

Once you have a list of names, it's time to make the origami hearts. You will need some squares of paper, coloured on one side, white on the other. They don't have to be red in colour, although obviously that's the traditional colour. You may want to have a few hearts already made, just to cut down the time required for making them. It also might emerge that the young person is not very keen or confident with this type of craft activity, and so having a few already made can be helpful. This enables the activity to still go ahead, with just the making element of it removed. Alternatively, you could make the heart but just leave the last two steps undone for the young person to complete. That way they get the chance to feel they have been part of the making, without the pressure of making the whole heart themselves.

Instructions for making the hearts

Fold and unfold the square in half from side to side with the white side on top.

Fold a little of each bottom corner.

Fold the bottom corner up to meet the middle fold line.

Turn the paper over so the coloured side is on top.

Fold the sides in to meet the middle fold line.

Fold the paper in half from top to bottom.

Fold down a little of each top corner. Press each one flat, then unfold.

Push in these top corners so they look neat.

Turn the paper over and voila, you have your origami heart.

You don't have to make the origami hearts, but, if you have a young person who would be able to and would appreciate this activity, then it can add to the experience and be an enjoyable and relaxing introduction. It's a good idea to get familiar with making the origami heart yourself before introducing it to the young person. Alternatively, as the instructions are clear, you can make one each, going step by step together.

On the front of the hearts, the young person writes the names of the people who have had a positive influence in their life. An alternative is to cut out heart-shaped pieces of card on which the young person can write the names.

Talk with the young person about each person and ask them what influence that person has had or what they feel they have given them. Inside the heart, you can make a note of what the young person has said about each person, the things that person has brought into their life.

On a table or safe surface, place a tea light in its holder and place the heart behind the holder, at a safe distance.

The young person can light all the tea lights and then dim the lights and reflect, just for a couple of minutes, about all the people who have loved them and had a positive influence on their life. At the end of the 2 minutes, ask the young person which feelings they have experienced in carrying out the activity. Many young people experience a sense of pride and happiness thinking about the positive influence that others have had in their life. Sometimes there is sadness as well, as some people are no longer part of their life.

Display the hearts in the young person's life story workbook in such a way that they can still be opened to see what is inside.

Case study

Curiously, the week before carrying out this activity with Ian, he had in fact set fire to some carpet in the home. After some discussion with the carer as to the nature of the activity and whether it was safe to go ahead with using the tea lights, we decided that it would be OK as it was closely supervised and, in a way, the activity would demonstrate the trust that we had in him to act responsibly with fire, that he was able to be trusted and that he had learned from the incident the previous week. Reparation and fire awareness work had been undertaken with him following the carpet incident. Ian was able to engage sensibly and found the session touching and meaningful. He said that it helped him to think about, and appreciate more, all the people in his life.

Session 10: The Team of Life, part 1: values

For young people whose love is football or any sort of sport/hobby, the Team of Life methodology (Denborough, 2008, 2018) offers a useful way of starting conversations that help the young person explore the stories they have about their life. As with the Tree of Life, this methodology allows the young people to give multi-storied testimonies of their lives (Denborough, 2008). Stories that acknowledge the difficult times, but also acknowledge the positive ways in which the young person and their loved ones have responded to difficulties and trauma. The approach was originally developed for young Sudanese people whose love was football (Denborough, 2008), but it can be adapted to suit any sport or hobby that the young person is keen on. The Team of Life will take up to three sessions to complete, as there are a number of different parts to it. The first session focuses on the particular sport or activity the young person is interested in and tries to help them to tell stories of the positive values they appreciate in that sport/hobby and relate them to the values that they demonstrate in their lives. I have used boxes to suggest possible questions, but this is not a script that needs to be strictly adhered to. Use the questions as a way of guiding the discussion.

You will need:
- Paper and coloured pens
- The feelings chart made in Session 1
- Working agreement.

Emotional demand: low to medium

You could do this one on your own with the young person if need be. Although there are no guarantees, this session, which focuses on their values using the medium of their chosen sport, is less likely to engender lots of uncomfortable feelings.

What follows should not be seen as a script but rather guidelines and suggestions for the course of your discussion. It might be that you spend much longer on one question and don't get on to others, and that is fine.

What you love about your sport

- 'How long have you loved [name of sport]?'
- 'Who taught you this love of the game?'
- 'Who introduced you to it?'
- 'What is it you most like about the game?'

Record what the young person says to these questions on a flip chart or on a piece of paper. You might get some answers along the lines shown in the figure.

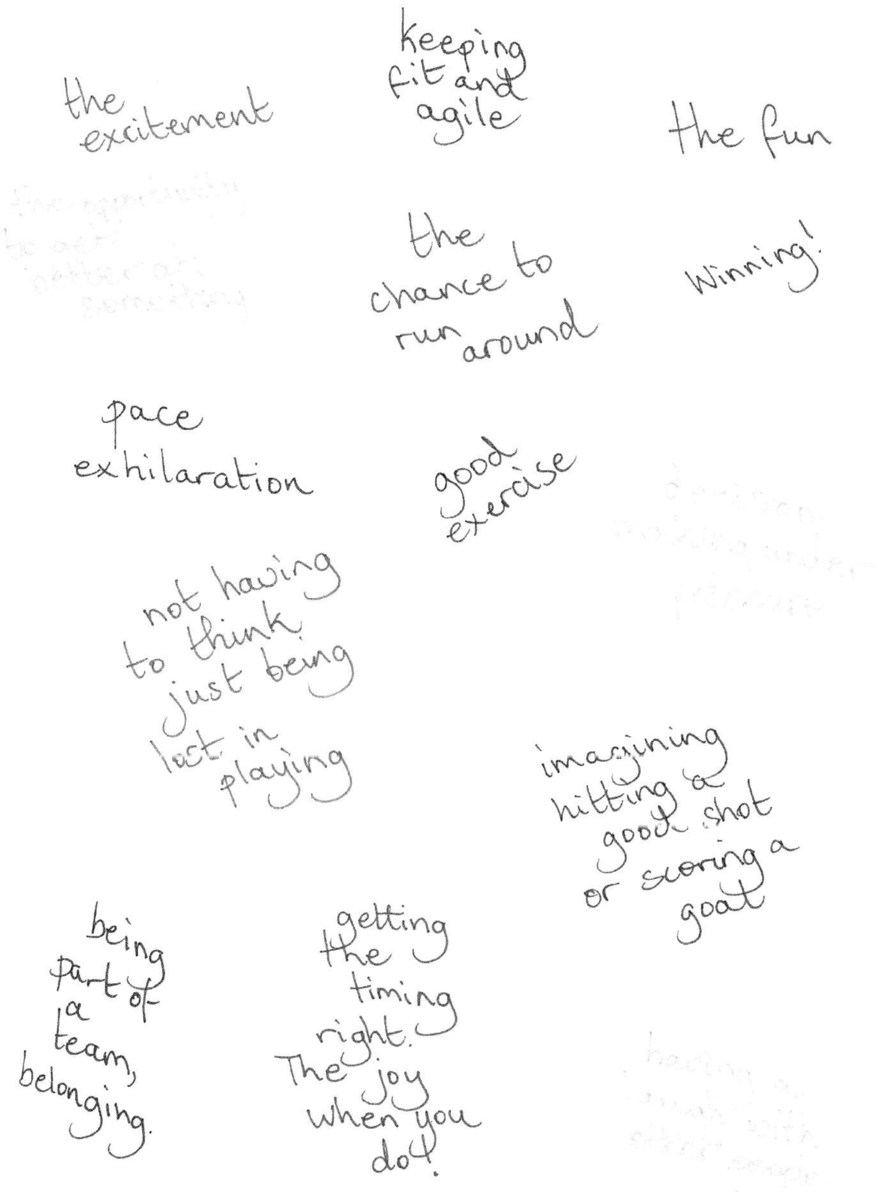

the excitement

keeping fit and agile

the fun

the chance to run around

winning!

pace exhilaration

good exercise

not having to think, just being lost in playing

imagining hitting a good shot or scoring a goal

being part of a team, belonging.

getting the timing right. The joy when you do!

You can then go into any of the responses and ask questions such as:

- 'So, having a laugh with others [or whatever they identify], is this something you value in other areas of your life as well?'
- 'Who taught you, do you think, about the value of fun and laughter?'

Favourite player/famous person in that area

Often young people have a player or person that they admire in their sport or area of interest.

- 'Do you have a favourite player? If so who are they?'
- 'What is it about them that makes them your favourite?'

It might be their skill, speed and so on, or the way they work in a team. This again leads to useful conversations to explore this further

- 'Is this something that you value in other areas of your life?'
- 'Where did you learn the importance of this?'
- 'Do you try to display these traits in other areas of your life?'

In this way, conversations that started about football or tennis or acting can lead on to discussions about preferred values in life.

Session 11: The Team of Life, part 2: identifying their team and goals

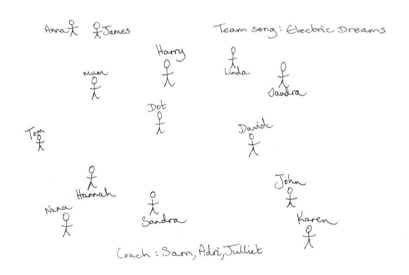

In the second part of the methodology, the young person identifies the team of people around them who are important to them, their Team of Life. It is helpful to draw this out using a map of the sporting area, or hobby, that the young person particularly likes. So, this could be a football pitch, a basketball court, a theatre and so on (see Appendix 4 for a useful football pitch outline).

> You will need:
> - Paper and coloured pens
> - An outline of the football pitch (see Appendix 4) or other relevant sporting area
> - Working agreement
> - Feelings chart.

As with the previous session, what follows should not be thought of as a script that needs to be strictly adhered to, but rather as conversation starters that take you on helpful pathways. Some pathways make take more time and exploration than others, and it is likely that you won't use all the questions. I'm giving you permission here that that's OK.

Team members

'We're going to think about some of the team members of your life. These can be people who are present now or in the past that have had an influence.'

Goalkeeper

'Who is your goalkeeper? Who looks after you, guards your goals, is most reliable? Who always seems to be there to protect you?'

Defence

- 'Who else assists you in protecting your hopes and dreams, in protecting what is important to you?'
- 'Who defends you when you feel others are attacking?'

Attack

- 'Who assists you and encourages you to try and achieve things?'
- 'Who inspires you to go for it and do the things that are your hopes and dreams?'
- 'Who encourages and challenges you to take risks?'

Other teammates

'Who are some of the other teammates in your life that you play with and whose company you enjoy?'

Coach

It's useful to remember a person could have more than one coach, and they may not still be alive.

- 'Who is it you have leaned most from?'
- 'What sorts of thing have they taught you?'

Interchange

- 'Are there some people who are a bit intermittent?'
- 'Are there people who sometimes seem to be on your team, but then are not at other times?'
- 'Are there some people who you see as being against you rather than for you at times?'

Stadium/sports ground

- 'Where is your home ground?'
- 'Where is the place that you feel most at home?'

It's important to remember there might be more than one place.

Team song

'Do you have a particular song that means a lot to you, that you might call a theme song in your life at the moment?'

People watching

> 'Who are your supporters, the people living or not living who are watching you and hoping you will do well?'

All the people the young person identifies can be written on a football pitch (or other relevant sport outline), such as the one pictured. A larger version of this pitch can be found in Appendix 4.

Goals

The focus here is on a goal that has already been scored, and so it precludes the possibility of failure. It also emphasises that goals that are scored are usually a team effort, and that everyone has a part to play, including the young person.

- 'Name one goal that you have been able to achieve in the last year?'
- 'How long had you aspired to this goal before you achieved it?'
- 'What help did you have from your team?'

Training

- 'How did you prepare in order to fulfil this goal?'
- 'How often did you do this training?'
- 'Where did you train?'
- 'How did you learn how to do this training?'
- 'Did anyone show you how?'
- 'Who assisted you in scoring the goal/achieving the ambition?'
- 'Who was involved?'
- 'Was it a solo effort?'
- 'Who encouraged you with tactics?'
- 'What does it say about you and your team that you were able to score this goal?'

Celebration

- 'How does your favourite team celebrate when goals have been scored?'
- 'How did you celebrate the goal that you achieved?'
- 'Who did you celebrate with?'

Future goals

- 'What is the next goal you are planning to achieve?'
- 'How are you training to do this?'
- 'Who are you going to involve in this training?'

In between sessions, the young person may want to share their Team of Life picture with another significant adult in their life.

Session 12: The Team of Life, part 3: tackling problems

This session acknowledges the difficulties a young person will have encountered in their life, again through the analogy of difficulties encountered in their sport or hobby.

> You will need:
> - Paper and coloured pens
> - Team of Life picture from the previous session
> - Working agreement
> - Feelings chart.

Emotional demand: medium

This session explores some of the difficulties and hurdles the young person might have faced often that were out of their control. Read through the session and use your knowledge of the young person and the sorts of things that are likely to come up to judge how difficult this session might be for them.

As with the previous session, what follows should not be thought of as a script that needs to be strictly adhered to, but rather conversation starters that take you on helpful pathways. Some pathways may take more time and exploration than others, and it is likely that you won't use all the questions. I'm giving you permission here that that's OK.

Exploring difficulty

- 'Tell me about a difficulty or area you needed to improve in your chosen sport/hobby.'
- 'How did you approach this problem?'
- 'Were other teammates involved? How did they help?'
- 'What skills did you use in overcoming the problem?'
- 'When did you learn these skills?'
- 'What does it say about you and your team that you were able to tackle this problem?'
- 'What tips would you give to other players who are trying to tackle a similar problem?'

Sometimes, even if we've got a really good team around us and we train hard and do all the right things, there can be obstacles in our way that are hard to overcome. Young people who have experienced trauma where they were not in control and didn't have a strong team around them understand this.

In football and other sports, there are sometimes things that make the game really difficult to play and seem to conspire against us. It can be useful to brainstorm the things that are out of the young person's control when they are playing their sport or doing their hobby. The figure has a few ideas to get you going.

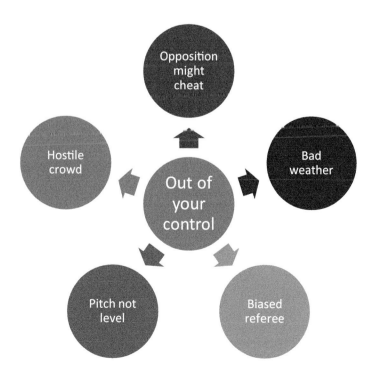

Discuss

> 'When it's like this, is it the fault of the team that they are not able to score, or if they don't do as well as they might have?'

Young people are often quick to acknowledge that, in these sorts of situations, it's not the fault of the team. So, then you can ask about the sorts of things the team do when things are not fair.

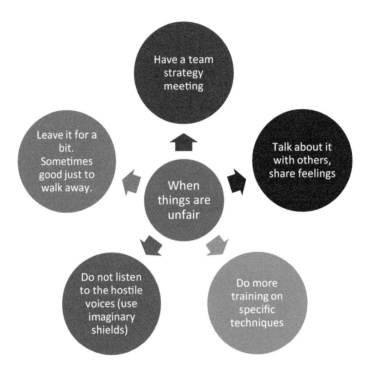

Just as in football or other sports, sometimes things are not fair in life, and we face obstacles.

> 'What are some of the obstacles that people face in their lives that makes achieving their goals more difficult?'

These might include things such as:

- Poverty;
- Racism;
- Being bullied/picked on;
- Violence;

- People's opinions/prejudices;
- Lack of suitable jobs;
- The political situation.

You can then ask:

> 'In these sorts of circumstances, is it people's fault that they sometimes can't achieve their goals?'

This gives you and the young person the chance to acknowledge the impact of broader issues on their lives. If the young person has not identified obstacles that they have faced personally, you can ask them if there are any difficulties, like the ones that they identified, that they have experienced.

> 'Are there any obstacles that you have faced personally in your life?'

This gives an opportunity to talk more personally about the challenges they have had in their lives, and also to acknowledge that many things will have been out of their control and not their fault, but will have steered their lives in particular directions, maybe stopping them achieving some of their goals.

Going back to the safety of the sporting analogy, it's a good idea to return to the ideas they generated about what teams do when they face such difficulties.

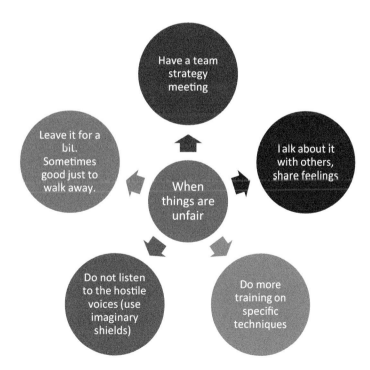

You can then go on to discuss if they have used any similar strategies when they faced difficulties in their lives.

> 'Have you used any of those tactics/strategies in your life when you have had difficult times?'

This may help them to see new strategies that teams use that may be relevant to their lives as well.

Looking beyond themselves

- 'Are there other young people you know who are affected by similar obstacles?'
- 'What about people who do not have such strong teams?'
- 'Is there any way you can support others who are facing difficulties?'

Certificate

It can be helpful to give the young person a certificate which summarises some of the things you have talked about in the session.

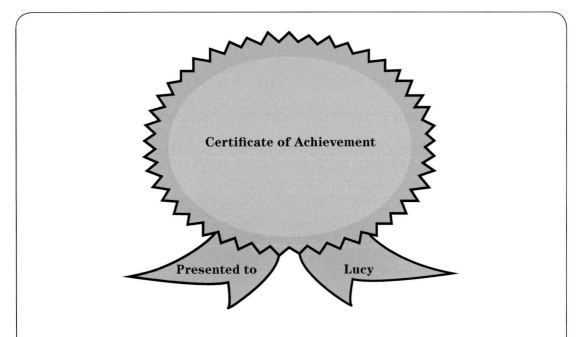

For not focusing on worried thoughts as much over the past year

Lucy would like to appreciate Tom and Alicia for helping her to talk about her fears and worries. They listen really well. She would also like to thank Sarah who taught her about writing down her worries and putting them in a box to help her externalise them and stop thinking so much about them.

Lucy's tips on dealing with persistent worried thoughts:

Try to find at least a couple of people who you feel comfortable sharing things with and force yourself to talk about the worried thoughts, even if you don't really want to. Get them out in the open, don't keep them all inside because there they can grow out of all proportion. Focus on the good things in your life as well and be thankful for all the people and things that you have in your life.

Session 13: Therapeutic stories

You will need:

- Time to prepare the story (this might be just the beginning part of it)
- Pens, paper or computer
- Knowledge of the young person's history, their story
- Knowledge of their interests, who their heroes are, who they admire
- Feelings chart
- Working agreement.

Emotional demand: medium to high

Hearing your story, or a story similar to yours, through the perspective of another character can be quite enlightening and emotionally hard-hitting. This might be a session where you definitely want to have the carer present with a comforting arm round the young person.

Young people often disassociate from the strong feelings that have accompanied their trauma experience. Intense fear and sadness are too much to experience for an extended period of time, and so, commonly, young people learn to endure the abuse or neglect, disconnected from their emotions. The young person can come across as being ambivalent or unemotional about what has happened.

Even with the help of emotions cards for expressing emotions, I found that Jonathan was unable to reconnect with his emotions around the trauma he had experienced. He was very focused on giving me the answers and responses he thought I wanted, rather than expressing any anger, hurt or pain. It was almost as if he couldn't allow himself to feel those things in relation to his story. Many young people may not appear to have any feelings about past events. Attributing the pain and emotions to a character in a story can help the young person claim and experience their emotions. Dissociation from these emotions serves a functional purpose, as it allows the young person to remain with an abusive carer who they depend on for survival. In essence, the young person sets aside the feelings of hurt, anger, sadness and shame in order to maintain their relationships with the caregiver. Even when living away from their abusive or neglectful carers, the young person may continue to idolise them and find it difficult to acknowledge the difficult emotions they experienced in their care.

Story and metaphor can help the young person to connect thoughts and feelings to memories. In their book *Connecting with Kids Through Stories* (2005), Lacher, Nichols and May describe how carers and professionals can tell stories in the third person to mirror the experiences and emotions the young person might have had. They describe this approach as telling 'trauma narratives'. A similar approach is also described in an article by Davies and Hodges (2017), and, along similar lines, but not specifically aimed at children in care, is the approach described by clinical psychologist Doris Brett in her book *Annie Stories* (1986). A chapter on this type of therapeutic story-telling is also contained within my book co-authored with Sheila Burton, *An Introduction to Emotional Wellbeing* (Shotton & Burton, 2018).

Third-person narratives provide safety. The young person can identify with the experience and emotions of the character, but the narrative remains being about another person, and so some distance is retained. It's important that the narrative is non-judgemental and attempts to try to understand and explain why the characters may have acted in the way that they did.

When we read or listen to a story, we often take on the perspective of the characters in the story. Neuro-imaging research supports this idea. Studies have found that, when people read a sentence about a person performing an action, the same regions of the brain are activated as are actually involved in performing that action (Buccino, Riggio, Melli, & Al, 2005; Glenberg, Satao, & Cattaneo, 2008). Studies have also shown changes in how we see ourselves as a result of reading fiction (e.g. Djicik and Oakley, 2014). Research suggests that reading stories can help us to identify with and understand others better, thus increasing our levels of empathy (Kidd & Castano, 2013; Johnson, 2012, 2013; Mar, Oatley, & Peterson, 2009). The young person can develop empathy for themselves as they look in on themselves from a third-person perspective, as well as perhaps developing empathy and understanding for other characters in their story.

Although a sense of safety is maintained because of the use of the third person, the young person will recognise the story and may find it difficult to hear. You may find that they fidget or are reluctant to make eye contact. This is normal and should be expected. The emphasis in the story should be on the resilience that the young person has shown through these difficult events.

A joint interactive approach

One way to approach this is to write the story together and do it in a way that does not seem too childish or patronising. It's helpful to write the first part of the story on your own, then introduce the idea to the young person, reading out the introduction you have created, and then start to add in ideas that they come up with. It is likely that this will take place over a few sessions rather than being completed in one session. The following example reflects the life of Thomas, a young person in care, aged 12. Like so many looked after young people, Thomas had multiple changes of placement. He spent the first 2 years of his life with his birth mother, before being taken into care owing to neglect. He and his brother were looked after by foster carers for 4 years before being returned to the care of their birth mum. After 2 years of further neglect, mainly due to substance and alcohol misuse, they were then taken back into foster care. Thomas was looked after for a further year in one foster care placement before this broke down and he moved to another placement.

I wrote this first part of the story and introduced it to Thomas in one of our sessions. I explained it reflected some of the things that had happened to him but wasn't exactly his story. I asked for his help in finishing the story so that, if he felt comfortable with this, it could potentially be used to help children younger than him in care.

> There was once a young fox, a vixen, who had been brought up very strictly by her parents. She had never had very much fun in her life and hated all the strict rules her parents imposed upon her. She ran away from them and found an old shed in which she lived. She made friends with some other foxes. There were lots of parties where the foxes would eat a certain type of leaf that made them feel woozy and not with it, happy and silly. The young fox discovered another fox whom she liked very much and soon discovered she was going to have a baby fox of her own.
>
> The trouble was, she was only a young fox herself and had no idea about how to look after a baby fox cub. The male fox was no help; often he would eat the special leaves and would become violent and mean with the young fox. He would bite her and bark at her. Sometimes the vixen ran away and left the little cub on his own. Often, because she had been eating the special leaves, she didn't make sure the cub had enough to eat or was warm and dry. The shed leaked and often smelt really bad because she didn't clean up after the little cub or herself.
>
> I wonder how the little fox cub might have felt when those sorts of things happened?
>
> The young vixen met another male fox and soon discovered she was going to have a second fox cub. Once again, the mother fox didn't really know how to look after her cubs, and often they were hungry or wet. They didn't know when their mother was going to be nice and give them food and when she wasn't, because she had been eating the special leaves. If they cried, they didn't know if they were going to be comforted or if their mother was going to bark at them and push them away. They were only baby cubs and didn't know that it wasn't supposed to be this way.
>
> They often felt very worried because of all this uncertainty and they didn't smile or laugh very often because a lot of the time they just felt worried. The fox cubs hadn't done anything wrong to be treated this way. It wasn't their fault. It was just that their mother didn't really understand how to look after fox cubs, and she was too caught up in her own world.

Thomas listened to the story with interest and said that he would have a think about how to add to it. He revisited it with his carer, but in the end he decided that he didn't want to add more or engage with it. Even though the idea that had been conveyed to him was that it was written in a style to help younger children in care, he still found the language and imagery too young for him and said he found it 'babyish'. This serves a useful reflection about getting the style of the story right for the age and interests of the young person. It's not always easy to get the pitch right. The message here is, don't be discouraged if the story seems to be disregarded or rejected. For Thomas, a different style of story was needed, perhaps using a real-life example. Thomas was a keen football fan, and so looking out for the experiences of a footballer who had grown up in care and told their story, such as Mark Bright, would have been a better way in. Perhaps, though, the fox story had not been a total waste of time; in his book, *The Uses of Enchantment* (1975), Bruno Bettelheim compares telling stories to the scattering of seeds, only some of which will germinate and grow. Some stories fall on just the right spot at just the right time, and the young person finds them helpful; sometimes, a young person is not ready to hear a story, or, as in this case, the story wasn't quite pitched in the right way for them to relate to it. Sometimes, a story can remain dormant, but then, at a later time, take on significance for a young person as it is seen in a different way.

Lacher et al. (2005) describe how the same story can be told in different ways, using different settings and characters and adding in different details. As the narrative is told and retold in different ways, the young person becomes more comfortable with the narrative. When the young person senses the carer's acceptance of them and their past, they may begin to reveal new details about their past that then can be incorporated into the story. The aim is to help the young person integrate their memories into a coherent narrative and shift negative conclusions they may have had before.

Holly listened to the following story told to her by her foster carer, Saskia. She had a few questions as it was being told that opened up useful conversations about how children deserve to be loved and cared for.

Molly and Sam used to have parties that were really loud. Sometimes, the police would come around as one of the neighbours had made a complaint about the noise. Because of the parties, Sam and Molly were often too tired to go to work, and Sam lost his job because they said he wasn't a good worker. They didn't have enough money and used to fight a lot about it. Nobody cleaned the house, and things got pretty bad in there; it wasn't a nice place to be. Sam and Molly had a daughter whose name was Hannah. Sometimes there was food to eat, and sometimes there wasn't. When Hannah was little, she used to join in with the parties and dance around to the music, which all the adults loved. Often she would wake up in the morning and find that Sam and Molly were still asleep. One day, she woke up and there was nothing to eat in the house, so she went to the door, and for once it wasn't locked. She walked into the town and then realised she was lost. Hannah was hungry and lost and felt frightened, so she started to cry.

'Aww poor Hannah, that's a bit like what happened to me, sometimes in my house there wasn't enough food to eat and I felt scared that I was going to be hungry again', Holly commented.

'So, what did you do?' asked Saskia.

'Well I had to go to the shop at the end of the road and get some bread, the lady there was really nice.'

Well, in this story, a lady came along and helped Hannah too. She phoned the police, and a policeman came along very quickly. Hannah told him she lived in a house nearby but she wasn't sure where it was. The police knew where she lived and took her home. When they went in, there was a big mess everywhere, with bottles and needles all over the place. Another police car came, and a lady police officer took Hannah away in her car. She was really friendly and chatted away, but Hannah was scared because she didn't know what was happening and what was going to happen to Molly and Sam. Hannah went to live with another lady called Sandra.

'Did Hannah get to see Molly and Sam again?', Holly asked.

'Yes, she did but they weren't allowed to look after her again because they didn't look after her in the way that children need to, and deserve to be looked after and cared for.'

'Was Hannah happy with Sandra?', she went on to ask.

'Well', replied Saskia, 'at first she found it quite difficult because it was all very new and Sandra had some rules that Hannah wasn't used to. But the good thing was that she read nice stories to Hannah, and Hannah got to eat her favourite meals, and there was always food for her, and they went on nice trips too.'

'I bet Hannah was happy with that', commented Holly, smiling.

Holly related strongly to the feelings of fear about not having enough food and remembered how that had felt for her. Holly and Saskia went on to talk about this more, and Saskia often reassured Holly that there would always be enough food for her, because children need food and deserve to be fed and kept safe and warm very carefully.

The story allowed Holly to process some of the events that had happened to her and the thoughts, feelings and experiences of her early life. Saskia's ongoing love and care, communicated very explicitly, gave a strong message to Holly that no child deserves the kind of treatment she received, and that all children deserve to be looked after with love and care. That she deserves to be loved and cared for is an important message for Holly to internalise. In communicating that what happened was not her fault, the story helped to decrease the anger, hurt and shame associated with a traumatic memory and allowed Holly to form new meaning from her experiences.

Real-life examples

It can be helpful to use characters in the story that reflect the young person's interests and the heroes that they have in real life; this works well for teenagers. Real-life stories of celebrities or sporting heroes that the young person admires, who have been through the care system, will have an authentic resonance that can be incredibly powerful. Some celebrities and famous authors have written books about their experiences; for others, there are interviews online that can be quickly found through a search.

Lemn Sissay (writer, poet and chancellor of Manchester University) runs sessions with young people in care, helping them to express some of their pain through writing poetry. His autobiographical memoir, *My Name Is Why* (2019), details his painful experiences of growing up in the care system.

Footballer Mark Bright has written his memoirs of growing up in a variety of foster families, *My Story* (2019). Mark and his brother had positive experiences of being fostered owing to the love and care of their foster carers.

'Baa, Black Sheep' is the title of a semi-autobiographical short story by Rudyard Kipling, published in (1888). The story outlines the abusive care that Kipling received between the ages of 6 and 11 in a foster home in Southsea. He also tackles this topic in his novel *The Light That Failed* (1890), in addition to the first chapter of his autobiography, *Something of Myself*, published in (1937).

The following list of famous people who have grown up in care may help you to find a real-life example of someone whom the young person might be able to relate to:

Kriss Akabusi (athlete);

Louis Armstrong (American musician);

Paul Barber (actor);

Frank Bruno (former world heavyweight boxing champion);

Mark Bright (footballer and television presenter);

John Bird (founder of *The Big Issue* magazine);

Dilly Braimoh (television presenter and producer);

Rita Mae Brown (American women's rights writer);

Catherine Cookson (author);

Charlie Chaplin (film actor and director);

Brian Connolly (comedian and actor);

Patricia Cornwell (best-selling crime writer);

Coco Chanel (fashion designer and perfumist);

Alexandra Danilova (ballerina);

Paddy Doyle (Irish author);

Barry Evans (television and film actor);

John Fashanu (professional footballer);

Justin Fashanu (professional footballer);

Antwone Fisher (screenwriter and actor);

Ella Fitzgerald (American singer);

Goldie (musician);

Cary Grant (American actor);

James Gooding (award-winning photographer);

Damien Hirst (artist);

Debbie Harry (singer);

Lennie James (actor and playwright);

Kathy Burke (actress);

Kay-Jay (pop singer);

Kerry Katona (singer and television personality);

Rudyard Kipling (author);

Lemn Sissay (poet);

Jane Lapotaire (actress);

Neil Morrissey (actor);

Marilyn Monroe (film actress);

Eddie Murphy (film actor);

Steve McQueen (American film actor);

Harry Martinson (Nobel Prize-winning author);

Bruce Oldfield (fashion designer);

Edgar Allan Poe (American author);

Richard Burton (actor);

Samantha Morton (Oscar-nominated actress);

Seal (singer);

Leslie Thomas (author);

Mike Tyson (former world heavyweight boxing champion);

Vanessa Mae (classical violinist);

Vidal Sassoon (hairstylist);

David Whelan (autobiographical author);

Gary Wilmot (comedian and entertainer);

Fatima Whitbread (athlete);

Malcolm X (civil rights activist);

Choi Yong Sul (martial arts expert).

Look for accounts that mirror some of the experiences your young person may have had, particularly accounts that express the sorts of feelings the celebrity experienced in those circumstances. In this way, the young person may be more able to reconnect with the feelings they had. It may help to normalise those feelings, and just knowing that they aren't the only one to have gone through such experiences can be a source of comfort. The fact that the person went on to do well in their lives is also very powerful and serves as an encouragement to the young person that, just because you had a difficult childhood, it doesn't mean you can't go on to succeed and do well in your life.

Summary

Stories can be written specifically for the young person, or biographical accounts can be used to help them understand and reconnect with emotions they had during difficult experiences. Stories are helpful as they are one step removed from the young person and so can be a less threatening way in, yet, at the same time, can be very powerful in communicating messages to the young person about the abuse and neglect not being their fault, about the feelings that they experienced and perhaps the actions that they took as being something others have had too. All of this can be healing and helpful to the young person. All it takes is a little bit of effort and the willingness to have a go, realising that we may not always get it quite right in terms of the story we choose, and that's OK. A different story may be what is needed, or moving on and focusing on other sessions from this book.

References

Atwool, N. (2017). Life story work: optional extra or fundamental entitlement? *Child Care in Practice, 23*(1), 64–76, 1.

Aust, P. H. (1981). Using the life story book in treatment of children in placement. *Child Welfare, 60,* 8.

Backhaus, K. A. (1984). Life books: tool for working with children in placement. *Social Work, 29*(1), 551–554.

Bandura, A. (1977). Self efficacy: toward a unifying theory of behavioral change. *Psychological Review, 84*(2), 191–215.

Baumeister, R. (2005). Rejected and alone. *The Psychologist, 18*(12), 732–735.

Baynes, P. (2008). Untold stories: a discussion of life story work. *Adoption and Fostering, 32*(2), 43–49.

Beste, H. M., & Richardson, R. G. (1981). Developing a life story book program for foster children. *Child Welfare, 60*(8), 529–534.

Bettelheim, B. (1975). *The uses of enchantment: the meaning and importance of fairy tales.* London: Thames & Hudson.

Bowlby, J. (1980). *Loss: sadness and depression.* New York: Basic Books.

Bowlby, J. (1988). *A secure base: parent–child attachment and healthy human development.* New York: Basic Books.

Brett, D. (1986). *Annie stories.* New York: Workman.

Bright, M. (2019). *My story: from foster care to footballer.* London: Constable.

Buccino, G., Riggio, L., Melli, G., & Al, E. (2005). Listening to action-related sentences modulates the activity of the motor system: a combined TMS and behavioural study. *Cognitive Brain Research, 24,* 355–363.

Camis, J. (2001). *My life and me.* London: BAAF.

Christie, D., McFarlane, F., Casdagli, L., & Fredman, G. (2016). Witnessing outsider witnessing: a reciprocal witnessing workshop with young people reclaiming their lives back from pain and fatigue. *Physical Medicine and Rehabilitation Research, 1*(4), 1–6.

Clarke, A., Hanson, E., & Ross, H. (2003). Seeing the person behind the patient: enhancing the care of older people using a biographical approach. *Journal of Clinical Nursing, 12*(5), 697–706.

Connor, T., Sclare, I., Dunbar, D., & Elliffe, J. (1985). Making a life story book. *Adoption & Fostering, 92*(1), 33–46.

Cook-Cottone, C., & Beck, M. (2007). A model for life-story work: facilitating the construction of personal narrative for foster children. *Child and Adolescent Mental Health, 12*(4), 193–195.

Cozza, S. J. (2006). Commentary on 'Seven institutionalized children and their adaptation in late adulthood: the children of Duplessis': case studies of the orphans of Duplessis: the power of stories. *Psychiatry, 69*(4), 325–327.

Davies, M., & Hodges, J. (2017). Relationship renaissance: the use of attachment-based narrative and metaphor in life story work. *Adoption and Fostering, 41*(2), 131–141.

Davis, T. E. (1997). Telling life stories and creating life books: a counselling technique for fostering resilience in children. *Dissertation Abstracts International Section A: Humanities and Social Sciences Volume, 58*(11-A), 4197.

Denborough, D. (2008). *Collective narrative practice.* Adelaide, SA: Dulwich Centre.

Denborough, D. (2018). *Do you want to hear a story? Adventures in collective narrative practice.* Adelaide, SA: Dulwich Centre.

Department for Education. (2011). Adoption: national minimum standards. Retrieved from DFE: www.education.gov.uk/publications/eOrderingDownload/Adoption-NMS.pdf

Djicik, M., & Oakley, K. (2014). The art in fiction: from indirect communication to changes of the self. *Psychology of Aesthetics, Creativity and the Arts, 8*(4), 498–505.

Elhassan, O., & Yassine, L. (2017). Tree of Life with young Muslim women in Australia. *The International Journal of Narrative Therapy and Community Work,* (3), 27–45.

Ellis, A. and Grieger, R. (1977). *Handbook of rational-emotive therapy: Volume 2.* New York: Springer.

Fahlberg, V. (2006). *A child's journey through placement*. London: BAAF.

Fivush, R., Haden, C. and Reese, E. (2006). Elaborating on elaborations: role of maternal reminiscing style in cognitive and socio-emotional development, *Child Development, 77*(6), 1568–1588.

Fivush, R., & Vasudeva, A. (2002). Remembering to relate: socioemotional correlates of mother–child reminiscing. *Journal of Cognition and Development, 3*(1), 73–90.

Freeman, J., Epston, D., & Lobovits, D. (1997). *Playful approaches to serious problems*. New York: W.W. Norton.

Gallagher, B., & Green, A. (2012). In, out and after care: young adults' views on their lives, as children, in a therapeutic residential establishment. *Children and Youth Services Review, 34*(2), 437–450.

Glenberg, A. M., Satao, M., & Cattaneo, L. (2008). Processing abstract language modulates motor system activity. *Quarterly Journal of Experimental Psychology, 61*, 905–919.

Habermas, T., & Bluck, S. (2000). Getting a life: the emergence of the life story in adolescence. *Psychological Bulletin, 126*(1), 748–769.

Hansebo, G., & Kihlgren, M. (2000). Patient life stories and current situation as told by carers in nursing wards. *Clinical Nursing Research, 9*(3), 260–279.

Happer, H., McCreadie, J., & Aldgate, J. (2006). *Celebrating success: what helps looked after children succeed*. Edinburgh: Social Work Inspection Agency.

Harper, J. (1996). Recapturing the past: alternative methods of life story work in adoption and fostering. *Adoption and Fostering, 20*(3), 21–28.

Henry, D. L. (2005). The 3-5-7 model: preparing children for permanency. *Children and Youth Services Review, 27*(2), 197–212.

Hewitt, H. (1998). Life story books for people with learning disabilities. *Nursing Times, 94*(33), 61–63.

Hewitt, H. (2000). A life story approach for people with profound learning disabilities. *British Journal of Nursing, 9*(2), 90–95.

Hughes, G. (2014). Finding a voice through the Tree of Life: a strength-based approach to mental health for refugee children and families in schools. *Journal of Clinical Child Psychology and Psychiatry, 19*(1), 139–153.

Jacobs, S. F. M. (2018). Collective narrative practice with unaccompanied refugee minors: "The Tree of Life" as a response to hardship. *Child and Clinical Psychiatry, 23*(2), 279–293.

Johnson, D. R. (2012). Transportation into a story increases empathy, prosocial behaviour and perceptual bias toward fearful experiences. *Personality and Individual Differences, 52*, 150–155.

Johnson, D. R. (2013). Transportation into literary fiction reduces prejudice against and increases empathy for Arab Muslims. *Scientific Study of Literature, 3*, 77–92.

Kidd, D. C., & Castano, E. (2013). Reading literary fiction improves theory of mind. *Science, 342*(6156), 377–380.

Kipling, R. (1888). *Wee Willie Winkie and other child stories*. Allahabad: A.H. Wheeler.

Kipling, R. (1890). *The light that failed*. Philadelphia, PA: Lippincott's monthly magazine.

Kipling, R. (1937). *Something of myself*. London: Dodo Press.

Kristoffersen, G. (2004). Life story work: an important, but overlooked, instrument. *Mental Retardation, 42*(1), 70–76.

Kulkofsky, S., & Koh, J. B. K. (2009). Why they reminisce: caregiver reports of the functions of joint reminiscence in early childhood. *Memory, 17*(4), 458–470.

Lacher, D., Nichols, T., & May, J. (2005). *Connecting with kids through stories*. London: Jessica Kingsley.

Mar, R. A., Oatley, K., & Peterson, J. B. (2009). Exploring the link between reading fiction and empathy: ruling out individual differences and examining outcomes. *Communications, 34*, 407–428.

McLean, K. (2005). Late adolescent identity development: narrative meaning making and memory telling. *Developmental Psychology, 41*(1), 683–691.

Mennen, F. E., & O'Keefe, M. (2005). Informed decisions about child welfare: the use of attachment theory. *Children and Youth Services Review, 27*(2), 577–593.

Morgan, A. (2000). *What is narrative therapy?* Adelaide, SA: Dulwich Centre.

Nelson, K., & Fivush, R. (2004). The emergence of autobiographical memory: a social cultural developmental theory. *Psychological Review, 111*(1), 486–511.

Nicholls, E. (2003). Model answer. *Community Care, 3*(9), 32–34.

Portnoy, S., Girling, I., & Fredman, G. (2016). Supporting young people living with cancer to tell their stories in ways that make them stronger. *The Beads of Life Approach, Clinical Child Psychology and Psychiatry, 21,* 255–267.

Rohner, R. P. (2004). The parental 'acceptance–rejection syndrome'. *American Psychologist, 59*(8), 830–840.

Rose, R., & Philpot, T. (2005). *The child's own story.* London: Jessica Kingsley.

Rushton, A. (2004). A scoping and scanning review of research on the adoption of children placed from public care. *Clinical Child Psychology and Psychiatry, 9*(11), 89–106.

Ryan, T., & Walker, R. (1985). *Life story books.* London: BAAF.

Ryan, T., & Walker, R. (2007). *Life story work.* London: BAAF.

Ryan, T., & Walker, R. (2016). *Life story books.* London: BAAF.

Shotton, G. (2010). Telling different stories: the experience of foster/adoptive carers in carrying out collaborative memory work with children. *Adoption and Fostering, 34*(4), 61–68.

Shotton, G. (2013). 'Remember when …': exploring the experiences of looked after children and their carers in engaging in collaborative reminiscence. *Adoption and Fostering, 37*(4), 352–367.

Shotton, G., & Burton, S. (2018). *An introduction to emotional wellbeing.* London: Sage.

Sissay, L. (2019). *My name is why.* London: Canongate Books.

Treacher, A., & Katz, I. (2001). Narrative and fantasy in adoption. *Adoption and Fostering, 25*(3), 20–28.

UN Commission on Human Rights. (1990). Convention on the Rights of the Child, 7 March, E/CN.4/RES/1990/74, available at: www.refworld.org/docid/3b00f03d30.html [accessed 5 June 2020].

Vermeire, S. (2017). What if … I were a king? Playing with roles and positions in narrative conversations with children who have experienced trauma. *The International Journal of Narrative Therapy and Community Work*, (4), 50–61.

White, M. (1995). Reflecting teamwork as definitional ceremony. In M. White (Ed.), *Re-authoring lives: interviews and essays* (pp. 173–198). Adelaide, SA: Dulwich Centre.

White, M. (2005). Children, trauma and subordinate storyline development. *International Journal of Narrative Therapy and Community Work*, *3*, 10–22.

White, M. (2006). Responding to children who have experienced significant trauma: a narrative perspective. In M. White & A. Morgan, *Narrative therapy with children and their families*, (pp. 87–92). Adelaide, SA: Dulwich.

Willis, R., & Holland, S. (2009). Life story work: reflections of the experience by looked after young people. *Adoption and Fostering*, *33*(4), 44–52.

Appendix 1: Tree outline

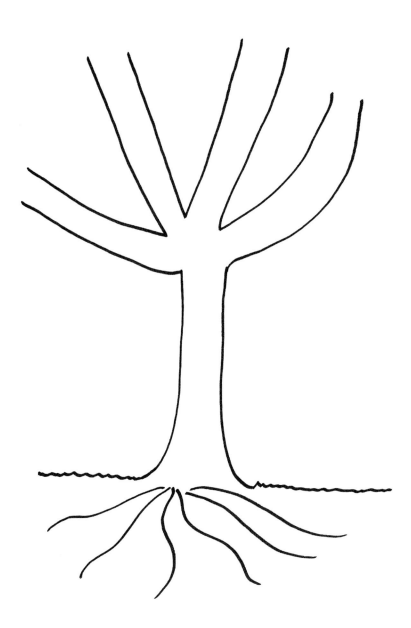

Appendix 2: Strength cards

Good at sharing

Good at looking after someone who is hurt

Lovely writing

Copyright material from Gillian Shotton (2021), *A Session by Session Guide to Life Story Work: A Practical Resource to Use with Looked After or Adopted Children*, Routledge

Copyright material from Gillian Shotton (2021), *A Session by Session Guide to Life Story Work: A Practical Resource to Use with Looked After or Adopted Children*, Routledge

Good organiser

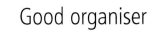

Good at maths

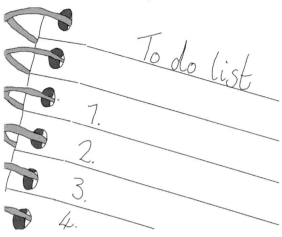

Good with younger children

Copyright material from Gillian Shotton (2021), *A Session by Session Guide to Life Story Work: A Practical Resource to Use with Looked After or Adopted Children*, Routledge

Good at tidying up

Good at encouraging others

Good at sport

Copyright material from Gillian Shotton (2021), *A Session by Session Guide to Life Story Work: A Practical Resource to Use with Looked After or Adopted Children*, Routledge

Copyright material from Gillian Shotton (2021), *A Session by Session Guide to Life Story Work: A Practical Resource to Use with Looked After or Adopted Children*, Routledge

Copyright material from Gillian Shotton (2021), *A Session by Session Guide to Life Story Work: A Practical Resource to Use with Looked After or Adopted Children*, Routledge

Appendix 3: Feelings cards

Copyright material from Gillian Shotton (2021), *A Session by Session Guide to Life Story Work: A Practical Resource to Use with Looked After or Adopted Children*, Routledge

Appendix 4: Jar of stones activity

Stone	Memory

Appendix 5: Team of Life, football pitch outline